DAWSONS

3/13   1135

£14 99

The Retail Handbook - Helping you achieve your Potential in Retail

Antony Welfare

The Retail
Handbook

Helping you achieve
your **Potential** in **Retail**

ecademyPRESS
www.ecademy-press.com

Foreword by Roger Best, Former CEO, Radley

The Retail Handbook - Helping you achieve your **Potential** in **Retail**

First published in 2011 by

Ecademy Press
48 St Vincent Drive, St Albans, Herts, AL1 5SJ
info@ecademy-press.com
www.ecademy-press.com

Printed and bound by Lightning Source in the UK and USA
Designed by Michael Inns
Artwork by Karen Gladwell

Printed on acid-free paper from managed forests. This book is printed on demand, so no copies will be remaindered or pulped.

ISBN 978-1-907722-36-3

A CIP catalogue record for this book is available from the British Library.

Contents

	Foreword	vii
	Preface	ix
	Introduction	xi
	Retail principles	xvii
1	**Know your customer**	**1**
2	**Know your product**	**17**
3	**Establish your brand and niche**	**31**
4	**Build a team to compete**	**45**
5	**Market your product and brand**	**59**
6	**Launch the business and Sell, Sell, Sell**	**79**
7	**Customer service is everything**	**89**
8	**Merchandise and manage your stock**	**97**
9	**Manage your information and finances**	**111**
10	**Build foundation for growth**	**125**
11	**Etail and Social Media**	**135**
	CASE STUDY ONE **Online retail case study**	**151**
	CASE STUDY TWO **Culture and values development case study**	**167**
	The Summary	177
	Top tips	180
	Acknowledgements	182
	About the author	184
	Testimonials	186

The Retail Handbook

Dedication

To all independent retailers and to the nation of shopkeepers

All my friends and family (A, B, C and K)

If you've enjoyed **The Retail Handbook**, then please

Follow **The Retail Handbook** on twitter
@AntonyWelfare or #retailinspector

Visit **www.retailinspector.com** or **www.retailpotential.com**
for updates and free downloads

Post a review on **www.amazon.co.uk**

Foreword

Sam Walton, the founder of the largest retail organisation in the world, said in his autobiography *Made in America*, "I had to get up every day with my mind set on improving something". You may not be aiming to create another Walmart, but any independent retailer starting out or looking to improve will find "The Retail Handbook" a very useful guide on how to do it. The book takes the reader on a well constructed journey through the key areas that need to be considered.

There is a good combination of strategy and 'nitty-gritty', with numerous common-sense tips based on insights from Antony's retail experience. Both the planning and the execution are well covered and each section has a helpful checklist of subjects to consider. The book is possibly unique in providing such a comprehensive practical guide to retailing in one compact volume.

Like any good business guide, the customer is always at the centre of things and I like the importance placed on values. The journey starts by challenging you to 'know your customer' and moves logically through the key functional areas of the business. There are strong sections offering up-to-date tips covering on-line marketing and social media.

Antony has set out to apply what he learned from his hands-on experience at large retailers such as Sainsbury, M&S and Dixons, to retail businesses of all sizes. The beauty of the book is that it offers the independent retailer the opportunity to exploit thinking and techniques often considered the preserve of big retail chains.

The case study covering 'Freshmax', Antony's recent retail venture, is fascinating reading and is a real-life example of how to put theory into practice. Antony shows he is passionate about his subject and this is why the '*The Retail Handbook* should prove relevant, positive and uplifting to any retailer.

Roger Best

Retailer with over 20 years experience leading consumer brands and former CEO of Radley

Preface

We all remember Tony Blair for some great moments – and not so great moments – during his time as Prime Minister. Some say that his most famous moment was at the Labour Party Conference in 2001, when his underarm sweat patch was the main topic of conversation at the conference, and one of his party even boasted that his drenched blue shirt showed he worked hard. This may be true, but the image of unsightly sweat patches has always been a problem.

This was the time before FreshMax Shirts – the only shirts that eliminate sweat patches – and the reason why I have written this book for you. In 2009, we launched a very successful online retail business to sell FreshMax Shirts to the world (and even Tony if he wanted one). We established a retail business which took a new fabric technology and science to a shirt, a new brand and a trading E-commerce website in only nine months. This business has since moved on, and the shirts are now being sold in Marks and Spencer amongst other large retailers.

It was during this period I decided to write this book – to help independent retailers grow their business and compete with the large retailers. I had spent 15 years in retail until I launched FreshMax, and during my time at FreshMax my eyes were opened to the issues and concerns that smaller retailers have, and the realisation that independent retailers could learn from the larger retailers and this could make them very successful.

I hope you enjoy the book, and I wish you every success with your new journey to achieving your Retail Potential.

Antony Welfare

The Retail Inspector
@retailpotential.com

Introduction to the Handbook

Welcome to The Retail Handbook.

This handbook is designed to take you as a retailer, or aspiring retailer, on a journey to understand how to run a retail business successfully. It is aimed at independent retailers wishing to learn the best practice from the larger 'faceless' retailers that we see on all our high streets, retail parks and online.

We cover the main areas of running a retail business and give you advice that will:

▼ *Improve your customer satisfaction*

▼ *Grow your product range*

▼ *Improve your sales*

▼ *Develop your team*

▼ *Sell more profitably*

▼ *Take the first steps to opening an online retail store*

This handbook will help you understand the process behind these areas, and introduce you to some steps for achieving these improvements in your retail business.

Even if you are new to retail, maybe you are wishing to set up a new retail business, then this book will help guide you through the areas that you need to plan and develop in order to achieve your potential in retail.

What is retail or retailing?

Here is the definition I found most useful:

'Retailing is the process of selling goods or merchandise to the final customer, and usually involves buying a larger volume of items and selling them in smaller quantities.'

Put simply (and in my words): the process of buying products, and then selling those products to the end consumer of those products.

In practice, retail is a very simple concept[1] – 'You sell your products at a higher price than you bought them, thus making a margin between the two figures'. On top of making a margin, if you manage your costs correctly, you will then make a profit, and this will enable you to grow your retail business and satisfy more customers.

---

[1] Join in Twitter conversations about Retail - All subjects are listed at the end of the chapter.

I often use the phrase 'it is not rocket science' when I am in retail – this is because I believe the statement is true. If you buy the products for your customers that they want to buy from you, and at a price they are willing to pay, you will make a profit and have happy customers.

The purpose of writing this handbook is to help you understand the process and strategies (the journey) that you can adopt to make your retail business a successful retail business, and help you achieve your potential in retail. The modern world is a highly competitive and challenging place. Smaller retailers are being attacked from all areas of their business world: there are new retailers taking your customers (i.e. the big supermarkets); new and existing retailers are setting up websites and E-commerce websites to take your customers. This is in addition to the growing trend of your customers becoming more educated, demanding and having a great drive for, and access to, knowledge about your products. They also have less time, and they know that the world is an extremely competitive market place.

On top of this, there is regulation and red tape, which is stifling your ability to be efficient and effective. The retail world is a challenge, but there are many things that you can do to help improve your retail business, and if you follow this journey you will see significant improvements in your retail fortunes.

This handbook provides you with a structured journey, with real life examples of retail strategies that do work. The structure of the handbook is aimed at delivering results for your retail business. Each chapter is a logical follow-on from the previous chapters and following the entire journey will improve your business.

▼ *To help you understand the journey the book takes you on, each chapter follows the same structured format:*

▼ *An introduction of the step in the journey you will be exposed to*

▼ *An explanation of the background to the step in the journey*

▼ *A guide of what you should do in practice to implement the recommendations*

The last chapter of this book introduces you to 'etail'; this is very important for all retailers, both now and in the future.

Etail is the word I use to capture all things that are retail, but not using the traditional physical stores – etail embraces the internet and uses all the power of the internet now and in the future[2].

Etail also covers new technologies such as smartphones, tablets and mobile commerce. Anything that is not a retail store, catalogue or call centre is very likely to be part of etail.

The potential of all retailers can be significantly enhanced with etail, and your time spent reading and understanding this chapter will pay you back with increased sales and customer satisfaction. The etail and E-commerce chapter gives you the ability to sell more products quickly, and to be able to compete on a longer-term basis with larger retailers that previously you were not able to compete with.

The final two sections of the book are real life case studies:

1) *The set-up and launch of a successful online retailer.*
   This case study covers the journey we took to set up a new
   online retailer that was retailing a brand new shirt to the market.

2) *The implementation of a customer-focused culture.*

This case study covers the details of how we established a customer service culture in a business that is not normally customer-focused. The business in question was a finance and customer service centre, which mainly processed information. I set the business up with the customer at the heart of the culture, and proved that any business can be developed and establish a customer-focused culture.

Both of these case studies take you through the journey the retailers followed, and gives you all the details of what they did and why they did it. These are very valuable references that show how you can implement the ideas and strategies contained within this book.

Throughout the book, I will highlight practical examples from the case studies, leaving the full case studies near the back of the book for further research and reference.

The main stages of your journey are set out below and start with my basic retail principles. After these, you will see the following chapters and

---

[2] Join in Twitter conversations about Retail - All subjects are listed at the end of the chapter.

the journey should be followed in this logical order. At the heart of the book is the customer, and knowing your customer is the first chapter.

▼ *Know your customer* – Understand your customers: know them, love them and satisfy them in every part of your business

▼ *Know your product* – Understand everything about your products and why your customers want, need and desire your products

▼ *Establish your brand and niche* – Establish a brand in a defined niche market and be known for this niche

▼ *Build a team to compete* – Build a high-performing customer-driven and motivated team

▼ *Market your product and brand* – Let people know what your product range is and why your brand exists

▼ *Launch the business and Sell, Sell, Sell* – Launch your business and your brand, then sell your products

▼ *Customer service is everything* – World-class customer service is your goal throughout the entire business

▼ *Merchandise and manage your stock* – Make your products look good and manage your stock as if it were cash

▼ *Manage your information and finances* – Make sure you know where your money comes from, where it goes and stay solvent

▼ *Build a strong foundation for growth* – A strong foundation is the key to long term success

▼ *Etail and Social Media* – Etail has always been part of retail, now is the time to embrace it [3]; make etail a major part of your future journey and success

[3] Join in Twitter conversations about Retail - All subjects are listed at the end of the chapter.

Introduction to the Handbook

Up to date information and social media – Join the conversation online

At the back of the book you will see the information on our the Flagship programme from Retail Potential: **The Retail Inspector programme** is designed to help local and independent retailers compete with the larger "faceless" retail businesses.

Using our tried and tested "Retail Checklist" process, together with customer insights we provide an assessment of the Retailer, to identify where they can implement best practice and ensure they can compete with the larger retailers.

With this programme, the information you can find on our website (**www.retailinspector.com**) and our social media channels, you will find lots of information to help you further your journey to improving your Retail Potential.

 In order to make this very efficient for you, and easy to follow, we have added the "Twitter" symbol to all the important quotes and information and the "hash tag" **#retailinspector**

Please use this **#retailinspector** to join in conversations about the themes and information in this book, and learn how to grow your business even further.

So remember, all posts and comments on Twitter, Facebook and other social media should end in **#retailinspector** to allow us all to follow the great conversations about retailing.

Join in the conversations about Retail on Twitter by using:

Retail is a very simple concept #retailinspector [1]

Etail embraces the internet and uses all the power of the internet now and in the future #retailinspector [2]

Etail has always been part of retail, now is the time to embrace it #retailinspector [3]

The Retail Inspector:
Retail Principles

There are many retail principles that have been adopted and developed over time. The purpose of this introduction is not to discuss these principles, but merely to highlight a few of the important principles at the start of your journey. This introduction will help navigate you to the right place in order to start your journey to achieving your potential in retail.

Principle 1

The customer is the most important person in your business [4]

The customer holds the key to every successful retailer, and to master an understanding of your customer there are many processes and procedures you could follow. This handbook follows a logical 11-part flow that centres around, and begins with, the customer. Based on 20 years of experience and a number of different retail businesses, this handbook will guide you through the journey to make your business customer-focused, and realise the potential you have to make your retail business a success.

Therefore, the main retail principle to master is the customer; the customer should be the centre of your business and everything you do must revolve around that customer. Knowing them, and focusing on them in everything you do, will help you grow your business and your team – The Customer is King.

> *"There is only one profit centre in your business – The Customer"*
>
> Tom Peters

[4] Join in Twitter conversations about Retail - All subjects are listed at the end of the chapter.

xvii

Principle 2
Retail is detail

One of the most famous principles in retailing is, of course, 'Retail is detail' – this is where the challenge lies: how do you become more detailed and what detail should you focus on? The answer to this question is what this handbook sets out to do: to help you start to address and improve your understanding of your customer, and the details of running a retail business. Every retailer must focus on the detail and get the detail right the majority of the time. Mistakes are OK, but you must learn from them and do not repeat your mistakes. Customers will allow you some mistakes, but too many will turn them away; understanding the detail is a key skill to master in retail.

Principle 3
Understand the 4 Ps

This is a very old principle but still has validity – most people have heard of the principle from school, college or university. This retail principle will help you understand the overall foundations of a retail business; the 4 Ps: Product, Price, Place, Promotion. These are the main areas you need to perfect for a customer, to provide them with the basic foundations of a successful retail business.

Product – *You need products that your customer wants to buy and a product range that will satisfy your customers' needs, wants and desires. The products must also deliver a profit for you to have a successful business*

Price – *Price must be consistent across the whole marketing mix and meet all requirements for your business. You need to price your product range at the correct level for the customers to be able to buy your products, and for them to gain value from your products. This could mean pricing high or low – this very much depends upon your customer offering*

Place – *You must provide somewhere for your customers to purchase your product, be that a physical store, a catalogue or an E-commerce website; there needs to be a place for the customer to visit (in person or virtually)*

Promotion – *Once you have a product – at the right price, in a place where the customer can access it – you need to tell them about this and promote your business and your products; make sure your customers know that you and your products exist and are available for them to enjoy*

Principle 4
Go the extra mile for your customer

This handbook will help you to understand this in detail, and how you can deliver this for your customers' world-class satisfaction.

Providing great customer service starts with understanding and knowing your customer (our first chapter); however, knowing them is the start of the journey and, as you will see as you progress through the handbook, you need to deliver more than just customer service. To be successful you must deliver world-class customer service; you must 'go the extra mile for the customer'. This principle is founded on years of experience with customers and working with many different teams that provide customer service. Having a total focus on the customer is the start, but to provide 'world-class customer service', you and your team must continually go the extra mile for the customer, each time delivering just a little more than they expect. Doing this each time you and your team interact with your customers will win them over and make them loyal over a long period of time.

Principle 5
Location, Location, Location

We mentioned Place above and the final retail principle I will introduce at this stage of your journey is: Location, Location, Location. History has dictated that this is one of the most important factors in the success of a physical store, and still to this day it will have a major impact on your success. The best location of your store will be dictated to by your brand and product strategies – i.e. what you intend to sell will affect the location of your store. For example, a supermarket operation needs a car park and a high fashion store needs to be in a high fashion area that attracts the right customers for the store. I would argue that location has less effect now than previously, due to two main factors:

the first being the flexibility of the customers; now we often travel more, to more varied locations than historically.

Secondly, and most importantly, the internet has changed our shopping habits and will continue to do so. The internet and E-commerce websites have opened up the world of 'non-geographic' retail – a retail world without the need to visit the physical store. The emergence of 'etail' from 'Retail' has been the biggest change over the last 20 years and will continue to transform retail over the next 20 years and more.

You will notice that 'etail' has always been part of the word 'Retail' - the journey from retail to etail has been quick, and we need to embrace the world of etail and ensure we understand its effects on our customers, today and in the future. The etail world is growing significantly and with new technologies, such as iPads and M-commerce (using mobile devices to access the internet and buy products), will continue to change the shape and opportunities in the world of retail. We discuss etail in much greater depth in the final chapter of this book and also in further products available from The Retail Inspector.

To get you started on your journey and to navigate your way through the book, I have devised a simple diagram that you will see at the start of each chapter.

The diagram opposite is seen at the start of each chapter and shows the journey you should follow in a logical order. The centre is the customer and knowing your customer is the first chapter.

Once you know your customer (after reading the first chapter) you can then move on to the next chapter which discusses your product. Follow the flow through the book and use the diagram at the start of the chapter to remind yourself of where you are in the journey, and what steps you have already completed successfully.

 Join in these conversations about Retail on Twitter by using:

The customer is the most important person in your business #retailinspector [4]

11 Etail and Social Media

2 Know your product

3 Establish your brand and niche

10 Build foundation for growth

CHAPTER ONE

Know your customer

4 Build a team to compete

9 Manage your information and finances

5 Market your product and brand

8 Merchandise and manage your stock

7 Customer service is everything

6 Launch the business and Sell, Sell Sell

The **Retail** Handbook

Helping you achieve your **Potential** in **Retail**

1 | **Know your customer**

Who is Your Customer? – The person who buys the products you sell for their end consumption.

Knowing YOUR customer: their lifestyle, habits, likes and dislikes is the MOST IMPORTANT element of EVERY successful retailer.

Your customer is the key to your future growth in sales and profits.[5] Understanding your customer will allow your business to grow with your customer and provide them, and the potential new customers they bring with them, with complete satisfaction for their lifetime.

This is the main focus of the whole journey to improving your retail potential and providing your customers with world-class service.

This section helps you to understand your customer, but the customer is not just mentioned in this chapter – you will find the customer is mentioned in every chapter (including the finance chapter) as they are THE MOST important element of your business.

The customer is KEY to unlocking your retail potential.

'Lifetime Value' of a customer

Knowing your customer takes time and effort, but it is worth every second of your and your team's time. Every penny that you invest in the customer will be returned in multiples if you make your customers happy and fulfil their needs.

[5]Join in Twitter conversations about Retail - All subjects are listed at the end of the chapter.

Remember: A happy customer will tell five people, whereas an unhappy customer will tell 11 people.[6] This is the most varied statistic in retail, but the moral of the statistic is to make your customers happy, and they will shop with you more and will bring new customers to shop with you.

Once you have a happy loyal customer, you can guarantee that the people they tell will become loyal new customers and they in turn will release more potential customers to you. We all like to moan, but we also like to tell our closest friends and family a great story about good customer service, and this personal recommendation helps to grow a good quality and loyal customer base.

In retail there is a concept called 'Lifetime Value' of a customer – this means looking at your customer over a long period of time. Think of your customer over the next five or ten years of visiting your shops and websites. Think about how easy it would be to sell those customers lots more products and services once they have tried you and liked your service and products. Making a customer loyal over the long term is much more important than selling them one or two products.

For example, if you run a clothes shop selling ladies fashion, your perfect customer would be the lady that buys a few garments every new season (and also tells her friends how good your products are).

If there are two seasons a year and she buys a top and a skirt each time at £100, in one year she spends £200; in five years she has spent £1,000 with you.

When she walks in for the first time, make her the most important person in the shop – look at her as a potential lifetime value of £1,000 plus.

How differently would you treat a £1,000 shopper versus a £100 shopper?

How would you set up your store and train your team to look at each customer as a 'Lifetime Value' not just a quick one-day transaction?

Here I have another example of 'Lifetime Value' for a local wine store:

A customer will, on average, buy a case of wine every three to four months. That means that an average customer will buy 48 bottles of wine in a year. At £7 for the average bottle of wine, that is a potential £336 of sales and with a margin of 35%, that is a potential £117 gross margin.

Know your customer

When you first meet a customer you should view them as a long-term customer with a margin value of £117 a year.

This value of £117 per year is what you can view as their Lifetime Value – each year you will make £117 from this customer if you keep them loyal.

Loyalty and Lifetime Value

Gaining a customer for their life time is an ongoing process that can be implemented in many ways – the main idea is to think about the total value the customer will bring to your business, and use some of the profits from that regular customer as an incentive or discount to 'earn' their loyalty.

You will need to 'pay' for the loyalty of the customer via discounts or other ways (see the next section where I talk about loyalty schemes for examples), but all of these will cost your business and you will need to make an investment into customer loyalty.

To keep them loyal, why not offer them a special offer; on their first visit why not offer them a 20% discount on the first bottle of wine (cost to you £1.40)?

Tell them that if they come back you will give them a further discount or offer e.g. 15% off the next bottle (cost to you £1.05).

The third time they come back, you offer them a volume deal – such as 10% when they buy three bottles (cost to you 70p per bottle).

You then offer 10% ongoing for the customer.

Let's add up the costs and profit in this example (I ignore taxes here for simplicity):

Visit	Retail Price £	Discount £	Cost price (65%) £	Margin £	Margin %
First	7	1.40	4.55	1.05	15%
Second	7	1.05	4.55	1.40	20%
Third	7	0.70	4.55	1.75	25%
Average	7	1.05	4.55	1.40	20%
Average of 48 bottles with 10% off	336	34.65	218.40	82.95	25%
48 bottles @ 20% off	336	50.40	218.40	67.20	20%

In this example we have retained the customer by offering a discount; this is not the only way to view Lifetime Value.

The total value of the discount in this example is: £34.05 (£117–£82.95).

This 'discount' could be given as a number of benefits to the customer: such as a free half-case each year (six bottles would cost you £27.30); a free wine tasting event every six months; or a number of free wine-related products (e.g. free glasses and decanter) every few months.

The example above is designed to help you put a financial value on each customer and give them special offers and events to gain their loyalty and make you the best return over time.

This shows that the '£100 Customer' should not exist in your culture, your team's culture or anywhere in your business. Thinking 'Lifetime Value' is where you need to start your journey today.

Please take a moment to visualise the Lifetime Customer of your store or your potential store – start to build up an image of them in your head.

Use the example above with your products and figures – what benefits could you start to offer your customer to make them a lifelong customer of your store?

Implement a loyalty scheme

A loyalty scheme is any type of programme or event that allows you to interact with your customer on a regular basis, to gain ideas, opinions and views on your store. It involves offering the customer something in return for their time and ideas – from money off to free tea and coffee.

Implementing some form of scheme that allows you to interact with your customer on a regular basis, to understand them better now and in the future, is important. This type of interaction is vital for continued success and growth of your retail business.

A loyalty scheme will allow you to understand what they like and dislike, what they want and do not want. How useful would it be to know what products you should buy for your customers and what not to buy? If you find out this information, you can buy exactly what they want, when they want it and know what price they are willing to pay for it.

A great example of a full service loyalty scheme is at Tesco. Tesco founded the Clubcard to help their understanding of the customers' purchasing habits, so they could market more products and sell more products and services to their customers. This was highly successful and has helped to result in the company leading the retail world in the UK and becoming the third biggest retailer in the world.

Their scheme is very simple: each time you shop at Tesco you swipe a card that adds to your personal database of information. Tesco then knows what you bought at what price and when. In return you get vouchers and money off future shopping. Tesco adds this data to your personal information and can build up a very powerful image of its customers. This allows them to target your personal interests and promote products to you that they know you will want to purchase.

Obviously the Clubcard scheme is very expensive to implement, but any retailer can still offer a scheme. We talked earlier about the wine shop discounting example which you could implement in any store as a tiered discount model, but you can easily implement a basic loyalty card.

I am sure you have been to a coffee shop with a loyalty card where you get a free coffee if you buy a certain number of coffees:

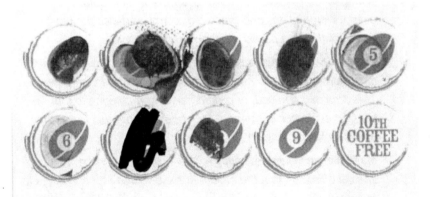

Or a discount voucher when you spend a certain level in a store:

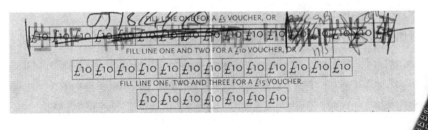

These are just a few easy examples that you can adopt to implement a great loyalty scheme in your store. With any scheme you choose, you must ensure you gather the customers' data as part of the process.

Gathering customer data allows for analysis of the customers' buying patterns and preferences.[7] This data can be used to buy your next range or promote good sellers/poor sellers or cross-sell a related product.

This customer data is factual and allows you to build a real picture of your customer and what they buy from you, in what quantities, at what prices and times. This data can feed all the future planning of your business, from the next season's range to the next year's promotional and marketing plan.

A good loyalty scheme would need to:

▼ **Gather customer data** – As much as possible, but a name and email address is a good start

▼ **Record your customers' purchases** – If you are able to tag their purchase on your system and find out what a customer is buying, you can build a very valuable database of their buying patterns

▼ **Analyse the total sales data** – You can analyse what products are selling in total (not by individual customer). This data can be used for promotions and marketing plans, and also the buying plans for the next period

▼ **Analyse the individual customer data** – Once you have the data at customer level, you can analyse what each customer is buying. This data can be used for promotions and marketing to that specific customer segment; if they bought a product once, they are likely to buy it again

▼ **Make the customer feel happy** – Offer a discount, VIP events or special offers, so that the customer feels valued and continues to shop with your business

Know your customers' habits – Visualise your customers

In order to understand your customer, and be able to sell the products they want, at the price they want to pay, you need to 'get under the skin' of your customer – really understand what makes them buy your products.

[7] Join in Twitter conversations about Retail - All subjects are listed at the end of the chapter.

To do this you need to find out about their lifestyle. Ask them, directly or indirectly, what are their interests, sports and hobbies etc. Use this understanding to model a picture of their lives – look for trends in the information. Maybe most of your customers like cookery, golf, Formula 1 or painting – if so then make sure your products and stores attract people with those interests.

For example, if your customer likes cookery, and you run a book shop, make sure the cookery section is clearly defined and that you promote the books, use special offers or events to make your customers happy. You can even partner with local shops or service providers to offer an even better service to your customer. For example, you could offer a discount with the local fruit and vegetable shop, or have a joint themed evening of cooking classes, with parcels of ingredients ready packaged for your customers to take away with your books.

To gather the customer information, use your resources:

■ *Your team and your stakeholders* – *Good team members will always interact with your customers, so ask your team what they know about your customers' lifestyles. There will be many areas of your customers' lifestyles that your team will know already; you need to help them collate these and discuss how these can help your business*

■ *Hold VIP events or local events* – *Hold a VIP event to gather data from your customers – offer some free drinks, nibbles and a discount in exchange for their time completing a short questionnaire. The questionnaire should cover all areas of the customers' lifestyle and be detailed enough to allow you to analyse the results and information*

■ *Set up a customer database* – *Collect your customers' email details when they purchase an item and email them a short questionnaire. Again, the questionnaire needs to be detailed, but online it needs to be user-friendly and take up no more than five minutes of their time*

Observe your customers:

▼ *If you run a local store, in a local area you should know your customers, and probably live near to them. You will already know what your customers' interests are – all you need to do is write them down. Take time out to think about what you already know about your customers*

> ▼ *If you are not local, make the time to observe the customers in your store – spend a couple of weeks watching the customers shop and interact with your team. Vary the days and times you do this and don't be afraid to talk to the customers yourself*
>
> ▼ *If you run an E-commerce website, you can employ research tools that can track your customers' movements into, around and out of your website. Tools like Google Analytics are a great start to understanding more about your customers*
>
> ▼ *Make sure that you employ data capture of their details to ensure you can understand and contact your customers in the future*

Understand where and how your customer shops

Finding out other places where your customer shops will tell you the other types of retailers they like and the type of products they buy. This information is powerful, as it helps you to understand what you should offer your customers more or less of.

There are many types of products you can offer:

> ▼ *Similar/complementary products to your competition*
>
> ▼ *Products that you know your competitors do not offer, yet you know your customer wants*
>
> ▼ *Products that your competitors offer, but you are able to improve the product or service for your customer*

For example, if you run a grocery chain, and you know your customers always shop at the local health-food shop, you may consider selling more organic foods, or make sure your customers know that you already sell these products.

Finding out how your customer shops is very important.[8] The times of just a physical store and maybe a catalogue have moved on significantly. Customers now use 'apps' on their smartphones, mobile phones, telephone ordering and the internet to research and buy products. You need to know how your customer shops now and in the future. For example, if you serve the under 25s market, you must have the latest 'app' to enable them to find your products, view them and order them if necessary. Likewise, if you serve the over-55 market, a great physical store experience with an informative website is a must (Fact: 'Silver Surfers' are the largest growing community on Facebook and for using the internet).

1 | Know your customer

[8]Join in Twitter conversations about Retail - All subjects are listed at the end of the chapter.

10

To find out where and how your customer shops:

- ▼ *Ask your customers* – *Ask them how they like to buy your products and where they buy them from currently*

- ▼ *Ask your team* – *A good, customer-focused team will interact with your customers and can easily find out this information from your customers*

- ▼ *Observe the customers* – *Watch what bags they have with them and what labels they are wearing. See if they have a smartphone or mobile phone when they are in your store*

- ▼ *Hold focus groups* – *Hold a number of focus group for a select customer segment, and ask them where they shop and how they shop. Find out how they like to shop now and how they think they will shop in the future*

Build an image of your customers

The purpose of this section is to build up an image of your customer – as clear and detailed an image as possible. You want to be able to describe every element of your customer and this will drive benefits in all parts of your business.

You are very likely to have a number of different customer segments, maybe four or more. With each type of customer segment, build up an image and name your customer segments. Sit down with your team and your data, to visualise what the types of customers are and name them – a person's name can be used to help make this process real.

For example, you may find that many of your customers are young males in the 25–35 age range and they visit your shop every evening around 6pm. You will immediately start to build up an image of these men, what they wear, the speed they shop, the types of products they buy. You could name this group – 'young male shoppers' or even a person's name that you know fits your desired customer segment.

Once you have defined your customer segments, you can then apply all areas of your business to focus on giving these segments world-class customer service. Give the customer segments the most perfect customer service that you can offer them, which they will appreciate and value.

Don't be afraid to be too niche ('niche' is explained as a small defined group with similar characteristics) with your segments – the more specific the segment, the easier it is to buy products for them and market to them. You could find your customer segment is even tighter than the example above and you notice that these men always wear suits, buy ready meals and use credit cards. You could tighten the name of the segment – 'young professional male convenience shoppers'. This process will help you define every part of your business and enable you to build a product range and process to satisfy your customer segments.

To build an image of your customer segment:

▼ **Analyse your data** – *Have a look through your existing databases of email addresses, names, orders and all other information you have at customer level*

▼ **Ask your teams** – *Have a 'brainstorm' with your customer-focused teams to describe and visualise your customer segments*

▼ **Build a visualisation of the segments** – *Look at their age, sex, profession, style, attitude, address, interests etc.*

▼ **Name the segments** – *Give the segments a name – this could be a real person's name if it helps give the real image*

▼ **Survey the customers** – *In return for a discount or special offer, most customers will answer a five-minute questionnaire, where you can gather all this information*

How to segment your customers? – Example table to complete (opposite)

In order to accurately segment your customers it is useful to sit down as a team and discuss the different types of customers you know.

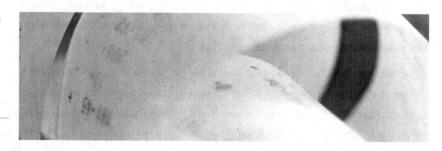

1 | Know your customer

Example: **How to segment your customers**

What do we know about our customers?	Results of Questionnaires and Surveys	Key Trends	Customer Profiles	Profile 'nickname'
Customer data – from the systems Customer feedback Staff feedback Sales trends in our area or market	50% of respondents had shopped at a local high street fashion store in the last six months Most had three holidays a year 20% never bought online 35% only came to the store to browse	Quality Time rich Cash rich Like to make a considered buying decision Research, but do not buy online	50yr+ Female Retired, but busy Mostly with grand-children Value the good things in life	Quality and considered
As above	As above	Fun Time poor Relaxation Entertainment Designer brands Online shoppers	25–45yr Male Work in the city Commute daily Like good restaurants Regularly buy designer clothes	High fashion spenders

In this example you can see that this fashion store has two distinct, but similar, customer segments. Both value quality and fashion, but they have differing priorities and buy over different periods of times (i.e. the first group take their time, whereas the second group are spontaneous).

Once you have the customer segments defined, draw and describe them – maybe on the wall or in your company internal documents. Make sure all your teams know who your customer segments are and what they look like.

This information should then be used every minute of every day, in every department – your whole business should now revolve around these customer segments:

You buy for these segments, market to these segments, merchandise to these segments, set your promotional strategies for these segments – these are the focal points for your business and the reason why you are in business – nothing else matters, only these customers and serving them the best you possibly can.

Case Study

FreshMax was a new concept and we had to define a target market segment to which we would start to market at launch.

We had to segment the market, in order to start a marketing campaign and be able to sell to our first customers. In theory the shirt should be available for every man and woman in the world, but we needed to target a very defined market in the beginning.

We defined our target market as: 'A shirt wearer in the South East, 25–50 years, works in an office and wants to look his best all the time'.

From this segment, we defined it further and focused our entire launch campaign on the London office workers in Canary Wharf. We realised that there are over one million men in that area each day. Concentrating on launching the business in such an area would be the most efficient and effective plan.

Know your customer

Summary

■ *Understand the 'Lifetime Value' of a customer*

■ *Know your customers' habits*
  – Visualise your customers

■ *Understand where and how your customer shops*

■ *Implement a loyalty scheme*

■ *Build an image of your customers*

 Join in the conversations about Retail on Twitter by using:

Your customer is the key to your future growth in sales and profits #retailinspector [5]

A happy customer will tell five people, whereas an unhappy customer will tell 11 people #retailinspector [6]

Gathering customer data allows for analysis of the customers' buying patterns and preferences #retailinspector [7]

Finding out how your customer shops is very important #retailinspector [8]

1 Know your customer

15

11
Etail and
Social
Media

1
Know
your
customer

3
Establish
your brand
and niche

10
Build
foundation
for growth

CHAPTER TWO

Know your product

4
Build a
team to
compete

9
Manage your
information and
finances

5
Market
your product
and brand

8
Merchandise
and manage
your stock

7
Customer
service is
everything

6
Launch the
business and
Sell, Sell
Sell

The
Retail
Handbook

Helping you achieve your **Potential** in **Retail**

2 | **Know your product**

The product is the physical item or service that you sell to the customer in return for value exchange (usually money paid to your business).

The product is the main element of the customer's journey – being the reason they interact with you. A customer only ever visits a store (online or offline) to fulfil a need, desire or want – no matter how great your customer service and marketing is,[9] a poor product will ultimately mean the end of the business.

Making sure you have the correct products and product range for your customer segments is the next step in the journey.

Decide what you want to sell

Even if you are already in business as a retailer, please follow these steps with your existing product and offer in mind. I am positive you will benefit from re-assessing your products and ranges.

In the previous chapter we built up a view of your customers and segmented them. We now use that basis to build a product range for those customer segments. Now you know your customer (or your potential customer) you can develop and design a range targeted to your customer segments. Finding out what your customer wants from a product and product range, alongside their needs and desires, will allow you to develop a product and service that fulfils those needs and desires.

[9]Join in Twitter conversations about this subject - All subjects are listed at the end of each chapter.

To develop your product range, you need to perform a thorough assessment of the market, your skills and your interests.

> The products that you sell should reflect the values and interests of yourself, and be of interest and excitement to you – you should sell products which you are passionate about. This passion will help you to sell and develop the products to your customer segments, in a profitable and fulfilling way. You also need to enjoy selling and running the business, so finding a product you are interested in is important – running a retail business is a 24/7 commitment, so you need to have a passion for the products you sell and the customers you serve.

When you assess the market, look for everything that meets your customer segment's needs. You can retail almost anything: fashion, food, wine, books, cars, CDs, cigars, plants – anything that has been manufactured needs to be retailed at some stage in its cycle to reach the end customer.

How to choose a product range

Choose your market	*e.g. Clothing, Cars*
Find your niche in that market	*e.g. Ladies, Luxury*
Research the existing product offering to that particular market	*e.g. Other stores – Online and Offline*
Decide on the overall product niche	*e.g. Formal Ladies Clothes, New Luxury Cars*
Design the product range to appeal to that niche	
Source the product for that niche	

Know your product

2

Once you have chosen your product range, one that is based on your understanding of your customer segments, you need to get to know and understand what makes your product unique – what are the benefits of your product versus your competitors.

Why should a customer buy your product versus that of your competition? Is yours exclusive? New? Better quality? Cheaper? Personalisable? Part of a theme/collection? Fashionable? Practical? etc.

You must understand what your product (or potential product) offers your customers that is different – Understand your product's USP.

A USP (Unique Selling Proposition/Point) is the general term that describes why your product is for sale and what your customer will receive when they buy your product. The easiest way to think of this is: what are the benefits of the product to your target customer segments?

All products are different in some way, even generic products can be retailed differently, with different retail propositions and services – again, understanding your customer segment will drive the USP for your products.

Understand your product's USP

To know your product:

▼ **Go out and research** – *Walk around your local high street or shopping centre. Find out what is in the market, what interests you, what your customers want, need and desire, what is missing or what products you could improve*

▼ **Use the internet** – *You can sit at home for hours and scan the internet for current products and new products – look at websites from different countries for latest trends and niche products that may not be available in your country*

▼ **Talk to your customers** – *Find out, from your customers, what they would like to buy, what products are missing in their lives and then research to see if you can provide these – you may even invent a new product based on this research*

Plan the sourcing strategy

Sourcing (also known as the supply chain) is the process by which you find, manufacture or produce the products you wish to retail. This could be as simple as finding a local wholesaler or as complex as sourcing the raw materials and manufacturing your own products.

Part of the getting to know and plan your product is understanding the sourcing strategy – the process whereby you work out how to get the finished product to your retail outlet/warehouse. This could go back as far as production and you could be part of designing and producing the product yourself or outsourcing the production.

Developing the whole supply chain is a normal strategy for new technology products such as FreshMax Shirts (a fabric technology company and online retailer), where we worked with an outsourced manufacturing partner to design the fabric, source the raw materials, weave the fabric, design the shirts, cut and make the shirts and dispatch to our warehouse.

Most sourcing for retailers is much simpler and involves finding a wholesaler or distributor. These 'middle men' will buy the products in large quantities direct from the manufacturers and sell them on to retailers in smaller, more manageable quantities. Palmer and Harvey and Makro are good examples of large-scale general wholesalers. Many retail product groups will have specialised ways of working and unique middle men, relevant to that sector in the retail market.

How to find a middle man

There are many ways to find a middle man – the easiest way is to research on the internet which businesses serve your particular sectors, e.g. wine suppliers, shirt distributors, fruit wholesalers, etc.

A great way to find new partners is through trade fairs which will be held throughout the year and specialise in your particular industry and foreign trade bodies, such as UK Trade and Investment (UKTI), who offer support and help for businesses wishing to trade internationally. You can also try your local Chamber of Commerce and Business Link.

Good sourcing will be in line with your values and principles. It is important to bear in mind the brand image and philosophy when you are arranging your sourcing. This is especially important if you plan to appeal to a customer type that values Fair Trade or organic farming. This is also true for sourcing products from middle men – you must ensure that the whole supply chain is ethical, safe and adheres to your values.

The final part of sourcing is ensuring that you will be able to get your products to your customers – make sure that whatever sourcing strategy you use, you are able to get the quantities you need, at the price you want, when the customers want to make the purchase.

Distribution and warehousing are the final part of the sourcing process and you need to decide if you will do any of these activities within your company or if you will outsource these to the specialists. There are many pros and cons to your own warehousing and distribution, and this needs to be understood at the planning stage. Most small retailers will leave this area with the middle men, who have the scale and resources to warehouse and distribute the products.

Planning the sourcing strategy would involve:

▼ *Finding out how your product comes to market now – Assuming the product exists today, you can easily research the supply chain that currently exists and adopt this process if it works for your product*

▼ *Use your existing networks and contacts – You are already connected to people in business, such as your accountant and your bank manager. Use your connections to find out how other companies source products and where they source them from*

▼ *Join networks and trade bodies – If you do not yet have a big network or you wish to learn more, you will find that most sectors of the retail industry have trade bodies or buying groups that can help you source your product; research such groups and make connections into these groups*

▼ *Plan your distribution and warehousing – Once you have the product sourced, you need to ensure you can get it to your customers. You may order in small quantities, have frequent deliveries, and have a warehouse or ship direct from supplier. All these are possible, but must be reviewed and planned in line with your customers' needs*

You have more connections than you realise

You already have all the connections and networks that you need to start – you may just not realise this.[10] If you are already trading, you are very likely to have the following people in your network:

▼ A bank manager

▼ An accountant

▼ A supplier (or a few)

These people will have many connections to other businesses – you need to ask for support and advice from these connections, and you will find that more people will help you and connect you with even more people who can help your business.

Other ways to develop connections would be through the support agencies in your area such as Business Link and Chambers of Commerce. These will have many different types of support and networks.

Set the pricing strategy

Setting the pricing strategy is an important part of developing your customer offer and your business values. The pricing policy of a retailer will not only affect the profits and sales, but also the perception of the brand and retailer.

For example, if I said Pound Stretcher and Harrods to you, you would immediately know that one is going to have low-cost retail prices and one will have extremely expensive retail prices.

Your pricing should reflect your business values, but also needs to be competitive and make you a profit – after all we are in this business to make money and we must make sure we sell the majority of our products for a higher price than we bought them for.

2 Know your product

Setting the pricing strategy should also reflect your plans for promotions and markdowns – some products are known to be discounted often or will be in end of season sales, but you may not want to have much promotional activity with prices (think high fashion – where they have very few sales and promotions on the pricing until the end of the season).

Establish a pricing strategy that provides the customer with the value and quality that they desire and are prepared to shop with you to receive. Go back to your customer segments and understand what they are willing to pay for your particular product and service.

To set a pricing strategy:

▼ **Price to make a profit** – *You must make sure that you have a pricing strategy that makes a gross margin, and that this gross margin should cover the overheads and make an overall profit (gross margin is the sale revenue, less tax, minus the cost of the product that you paid the supplier)*

▼ **Price for your market** – *Set your prices in line with your competition, understand where your customers shop and price accordingly*

▼ **Price for promotions and markdowns** – *Make sure you set the price to take into account any promotions and any markdowns you may wish to (or be forced to) implement. Supermarkets use a 'loss leader' strategy where they will purposely make a loss on some products in order to attract you to the store and buy more of their range*

▽ *Set a gross margin target* – *There are two ways to do this:*

1 *Set and calculate a percentage margin that you wish to achieve for each product or range, e.g. my business wants to make 40% margin on all shirts.*

This helps the buying process and negotiations, as you can work back from what retail price you wish to sell the product at, and therefore what the maximum buying price will be.

For example, we wish to sell our shirts for £50 (ex tax) and I want to make 40% margin to cover my costs – I need to make £20 gross margin, so the maximum I can buy the product for would be £30.

£50

40% Margin

Need this as I have a cost base of 20% due to high street location, for example

60% x £50 = £30

Cost price is therefore no more than £30

2 *Set a markup ratio or percentage you want to achieve for each product or product range, e.g. I would like to make 100% markup on the buying price.*

For example, I buy a shirt at £20 delivered to my warehouse, I will then sell this for £40 minimum

£60 minimum retail price

£30 is the markup I need to make per item to cover costs and make a profit

£30 is what I bought it at

Establish your quality values

Your product range will reflect your business's quality values and that of your brand. Once you understand your customer segments, you will understand what level of quality you will need to put in place. This will then drive your product quality level.

Your product quality will fall into three main categories: High, Medium and Low quality. All three are successful retail models and all three have the potential to make retailers good profits.

There is a three-way trade-off with quality, volume and price:

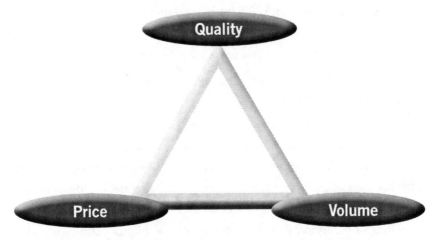

In this diagram you will need to work out where to position your product range within the three complimentary elements.

The three main categories:

1. *Low Quality = High Volume = Low Price – You need to sell a large volume of low-priced, low-quality items to make a return, but you will adjust down your customer service and added value services accordingly.*

2. *Medium Quality = Medium Volume = Medium Price – Mid-range retailers and businesses sell a good quality product at a good price and achieve a good volume.*

3. *High Quality = Low Volume = High Price – The higher the price and quality, the lower the volume and the possible customer base – Harrods have a lot fewer customers buying products than Tesco on the same day with the same sized store. However, most people cannot afford to shop in Harrods daily (or even yearly) but they can shop in Tesco daily.*

Design and develop the ranges

Once you have established your product area, your pricing strategy, your quality values and your brand values (see later chapter on branding), you can develop your product range.

Developing the product range involves taking time to plan what products you will sell from your desired product category. You will need to develop a product range that achieves what your customers would like and achieves the best profits and value for your business.

Think about the range as a customer segment – what will they want to see in the range? How will you lay out the range? Will it be a seasonal product range? Look at the range in total. For example, if you decided to sell laptops, think about the full range and all the accessories and related products you will need; with a laptop you will need a mouse, camera, carrying-case and maybe even a printer. Providing the customer with a total experience will be very beneficial, and very lucrative if you give the customer a full service offer of products and related products.

To create and develop the range:

▽ **Ask your customers** – *Hold product reviews and focus groups. Sit down with a few customers and discuss the ideas, even show them a few diagrams/videos/images of what the products will look and feel like*

▽ **Ask the experts** – *Work with creative product designers to focus the range on exactly what your customers would like*

▽ **Manage the total margin** – *Think about a product range in total and make sure you achieve the overall margin you need. For example, you may have loss-leaders to drive footfall or you may wish to have all products making roughly the same margins*

▽ **Manage additional products and cross-sales** – *Providing a full service offer of products is important for success. In the laptop example you may make more margin from the accessories than you do from the laptop sold alone*

▽ **Vary the range** – *Think about a full range offer – you may be known for high-quality shoes, but you could also sell shoe polish, shoe laces, socks and even shoe racks. Make sure the range does not creep too much, but added products that complement your range are an easy way to increase sales and profits*

Know your product

2

Summary

- *Decide what products you want to sell*
- *Plan the sourcing (supply chain) strategy*
- *Set the pricing strategy and policy*
- *Establish your quality values*
- *Design and develop the ranges*

 Join in the conversations about Retail on Twitter by using:

A customer only ever visits a store to fulfil a need, desire or want – no matter how great your customer service #retailinspector [9]

You already have all the connections and networks that you need to start – you may just not realise this #retailinspector [10]

2 | Know your product

The Retail Handbook

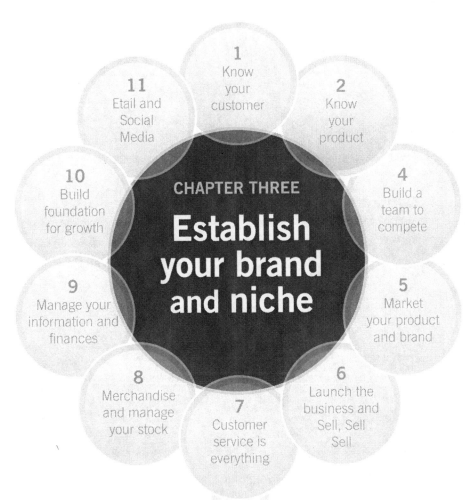

11
Etail and
Social
Media

1
Know
your
customer

2
Know
your
product

10
Build
foundation
for growth

CHAPTER THREE

**Establish
your brand
and niche**

4
Build a
team to
compete

9
Manage your
information and
finances

5
Market
your product
and brand

8
Merchandise
and manage
your stock

7
Customer
service is
everything

6
Launch the
business and
Sell, Sell
Sell

The
Retail
Handbook

Helping you achieve your **Potential** in **Retail**

3 | Establish your brand and niche

Establishing your brand and finding your niche follows on from understanding your customer segments, and works alongside developing your product.

Your niche is the area of the market in which you operate and this can be as narrow as 'Retail of the best flowers to people who are getting married' or 'Retailing shoes to the city worker' or as wide as 'Selling good fruit and vegetables to my local market'. A niche allows you to develop a very strong marketing campaign, and enables you to really understand your customer segments – the more defined the niche, the easier it will be to retail to your customers, and the easier it will be to make money.

Your brand is your image and values – it is the way you act, communicate and the way your business is perceived. It is what your business 'stands for' and is reflected in every single part of the business – from the name of the company, the colour of the logo, the type of bags, to the way your team interacts with your customers and suppliers.

Find your niche in the market

This takes time to find out where you 'fit' into the market. As we discussed in the previous chapter, you need to find a product range and establish your niche for that product range.

Finding a niche in the market means researching the part of the market that interests you and your customers, and breaking that down to a defined section. Understanding what is the USP of your product in the market, and how that translates into a recognisable niche for your customers will help you define your niche.

This part of the niche development is focused on the customer side of the equation – you need to look at your chosen product and product range from the eyes of your customers, and establish what they like about your product and how they would see that as a niche in the market.

I talk of a narrow and small niche because this is much easier for small companies to start with, but very successful large companies adopt this exact same process. Apple has a very clear niche, for easy to use 'gadgets' that are 'cool' to own – this is a now very large niche, but nevertheless this is their niche.

Finding your niche in the market works alongside the product development process and as such you follow a similar process:

▼ *Go out and research the market – Walk around your local high street or shopping centre. Find out what market niches there are for your product. How do customers currently see your product in the market and where do they purchase these products from now?*

▼ *Use the internet to find where your niche would work – Have a look at where the product is currently sold and what the market looks like – is there a clear niche that you can see for your product?*

▼ *As a customer, think of what your niche would be defined as and what you would need to offer the customers. For example, if you were a florist and said your niche was 'Selling flowers' you would find hundreds of companies doing this on every street corner and all over the internet space. If, however, you find your customers are normally people who are attending weddings or parties, you could set your niche as 'Retail of the best flowers to people who are getting married'. This helps you target very specific people with a high-quality tailored service just for them, at the time they need to use your products*

▼ *Talk to your customers – Find out from your customers what they see as a good market niche and what products they would like to see in this market*

Develop your brand and brand values

What is a brand? Your brand is the identity of your business and your products, and often includes physical words, colours and logos.[11] Most of the brand is intangible, and therefore hard to understand. This section talks you through an understanding of what a brand is and gives you a practical process to follow in order to establish and develop your brand.

Your brand and the values your brand stands for span every part of your company. As such, the brand must be thought through and developed to a very detailed level. This is part of the process to grow and develop your business over time, but you must start with a vision of what the values are and this is where the brand journey begins.

Your brand is 'living and breathing' and, as such, needs to be treated with care, and allowed to grow and develop as your customers and your team grow and develop.

Your brand is in every part of your business, from the culture and ways of working to your logo and your packaging. It can be seen inside all the people in your business and in all the products you sell.

Take time to understand your customer segments first and develop the products for these customer segments. Then, work on your niche to identify where you 'fit' in the market. Once these processes are in progress you can then start to develop the brand around these.

To develop the brand and brand values:

1. *Gather together your team and spend at least one day brainstorming WHAT the brand means to them; talk about your and your team's:*

    Feelings, images, looks, customers, products, people, colours, emotions, smells, sounds etc.

2. *Use these words and images to form a vision board of the brand. This could be pages of pictures and words on the wall or a number of statements that come out from Part 1 – at this stage I would propose the use of external agencies to help you through the process, but you could do this yourself.*

[11]Join in Twitter conversations about Retail - All subjects are listed at the end of the chapter.

An example of a vision board we used in one of my previous businesses is below.

As you can see, it holds different images and pictures which all form a small part of the brand and the image I wanted to create for this particular company.

The addition of characters, with the static images, helped create the brand values, look and feel.

3. *With the creative partner (or as a team independently), talk through your team's 'vision' for the brand and allow them to ask you questions regarding the make-up of the brand in your mind. Again, always remember the customer segments you are targeting.*

4. *Ask for a number of possible storyboards and logos/imagery to be developed (and a brand name if you do not have one) or develop a couple of options for yourself and your team.*

5. *Review these options and allow the team to 'feel' which brand and imagery is best – when you see the possible imagery for your brand (logo, colours and name), one or two will immediately 'work' for you and your team; these should then be further explored and understood why and what you like about them.*

6. *Once you have agreed on the brand and imagery (this will no doubt take three or four updates), you can then start to develop your business around the brand values.*

The brand values are sets of statements that will help you, your team and your customers 'feel' the brand you have created. These values will drive your identity and help establish your USP in your niche.

3 Establish your brand and niche

How we branded FreshMax Shirts

In 2009 we already had the name 'FreshMax', and we had a blue and white logo designed a few years previously. This logo was used solely in the discussions with other retailers, whilst attempting to persuade them to sell our SmartWeave fabric in their shirts.

We quickly realised we needed a totally new brand and in the beginning we thought we wanted a new name and brand. The previous image was 'sterile' and did not stand for anything – it was literally the name written in blue and white. The imagery and brand values were business- and technology-focused – we needed a high-quality, customer-facing brand.

We tested the idea of a new brand and new name with a number of different agencies, and some even came up with new names for the business, but we quickly realised it was best to stick to the original name and develop a new brand image and values for FreshMax.

Eventually, we employed a creative agency whose brief it was to create a customer-facing brand for FreshMax and help explain the difference between the fabric business and the FreshMax brand as a shirt company.

The main goal was to keep the fabric brand separate from the shirts brand, so that we could sell the fabric to other retailers. The creative agency soon came up with FreshMaxShirts for the shirts and 'SmartWeave' for the fabric.

During a two-week process, we talked about what we wanted from the brand and what our target market looked like. We had images and talked about what the customers' life was like, i.e. where they shopped, where they worked, their hobbies and the newspapers they read. From this the creative team presented three possible images and logos for FreshMaxShirts and the one we use now immediately made the right impression with all three directors.

The chosen image is below:

Over the following few months we developed a set of Brand Guidelines that covered:

▽ **Our Brand** – *An introduction to the brand and what it was introducing to the world*

▽ **Before and After** – *What the world was like before the brand was developed and what the brand will bring to the world*

▽ **The Brand Proposition** – *An explanation of the product ranges and a brief outline of their USP*

▽ **The Brand Impact** – *The impact and level we were trying to achieve via the brand*

3 Establish your brand and niche

▼ ***Our Customers*** – *The types of customers our brand targets and some information about them*

▼ ***The Brand Statement*** – *The words used to describe the brand to the outside world*

▼ ***Tone of Voice*** – *How we should communicate with our customers and business partners*

▼ ***Brand Name Usage*** – *How and where we could use the brand name and in what formats*

▼ ***Brand Phrases*** – *These are statements that help people understand the brand and what it stands for*

▼ ***Brand Values*** – *The deep values and meanings of the brand*

▼ ***Brand Appearance*** – *What the brand should look and appear like in all its differing uses*

▼ ***Visual Identity*** –

- **The logo**
  - *the use of the logo in all its allowable formats*
  - *the colour schemes and palettes*

- **Exclusion zones**
  - *where the logo should not be used*

- **Imagery**
  - *the photography and images that should be associated with the brand*

All of this work was documented in the Brand Guidelines which was then used to brief all the partners of our business; it was the document that communicated the heart and culture of the business. From the advertising agency to the shirt manufacturers, we made sure all the business partners understood the brand values and, more importantly, who our target customer was.

For a more detailed explanation of how the development of FreshMaxShirts progressed, please see the FreshMaxShirts Case Study in this book.

Develop the brand 'voice' and 'imagery'

Once you have created the brand and the brand values, you will also be in the process of creating the images for your brand. This is where you can develop ways to help your brand live and breathe and come alive in your team.

Once the brand values are established, you and your team must consistently 'talk' with the brand language and the brand voice. This means all communications from now on will be in line with your brand values and images. You will have a certain tone of voice, a certain colour scheme and certain images that represent your brand.

A great brand is known for very simple execution – we all know the Apple logo, we know who owns the golden arches logo and we know which sports company uses a tick logo. Of course, this has also taken many years of development and a huge global presence but, as we have shown with FreshMax, a small business can build a great brand and imagery.

Branding will cover EVERY part of your business, such as:

▼ *Physical branding* - *name, logo and colours*

▼ *Iconography and everlasting logos* (*e.g. the Nike tick*)

▼ *Collateral* - *bags and labels*

▼ *Communications* - *email signatures, business cards, letterheads, email templates and website formats*

▼ *The 'way' you communicate* *with your customer segments (happy, confident, clear, succinct etc.)*

▼ *The service experience* – *the bags you use, the fitting rooms and the customer service experience*

Decide on the channels of operation

The channel of operation is the place at which you will do business with your customer; this will be affected by your brand values and your brand values will be influenced significantly by your place of operation.

There are two main channels of operation: offline (physical locations) and online.

Offline (physical locations) are the locations that we have been using to retail products for hundreds of years. We now have many more exciting options than the local high street, but they all consist of a physical presence of products and a team to physically to sell these products.

The location of the store affects the brand and the types of customers that use your store and these must be aligned.

The main physical store options are:

▼ *High street*

▼ *In-town shopping centre*

▼ *Secondary high street location (just off the main shopping area)*

▼ *Out of town – retail park*

▼ *Out of town – supermarket/hypermarket*

▼ *Out of town – stand-alone store*

▼ *Drive-through outlets*

▼ *Motorway services and travel stations*

▼ *Industrial parks (near offices and office workers)*

All of these locations are tried and tested retail outlets; some will be relevant to your business and others will not. There will always be a number of options that you can use, and you may choose more than one channel of operation.

Online retail consists of an E-commerce website where customers can see your products online and purchase them for delivery to their home or office. Online is also expanding into different offerings:

▼ *Online E-commerce site*

▼ *Auction Site*

▼ *M-commerce – Shopping using your mobile phone*

▼ *'Apps' – using applications on your smartphone to shop anywhere at any time*

▼ *Social media*

▼ *Catalogue and Direct Mail leaflets etc. Catalogue selling and direct marketing has been used for a number of years, and most of these channels are now used to support a website and E-commerce operation*

And of course you should offer customers both online and offline – this is called multi-channel and this is where retailers must move to in the future in order to be competing successfully with other retailers (especially the multi-national larger retailers).

Multi-channel retailing is normally described as retailing via a number of distribution channels, such as via a store, a catalogue and via an online presence.

Your choice of channel is determined by:

▼ **Product** – *The characteristics of the product will mean a certain channel will be applicable or not. For example, is the product perishable? Of high value? Needs to be tested or tried on?*

▼ **Customers** – *How do they want to shop for your product and service? For example, can they travel out of town? Do they have a smartphone? etc.*

▼ **Competitors** – *You need to sell your products in a similar way to your competition, unless your USP is a different sales channel. Customers tend to shop for similar products in similar ways so you need to have at least one channel of operation that is the same as your competition*

▼ **Costs to retail** – *Understanding your gross margins and the cost of retailing via a certain channel is very important to your profit line. For example, does your business model, in particular your margin, allow for an expensive high street position? Do you need to offer lower prices? Do you offer high personal service?*

▼ **Accessibility** – *Understanding how accessible your channel is to your customer segment. Do your customers need parking? Do your customers have internet access?*

▼ **Experience** – *You need to remember your values and how you want your brand to be experienced by the customer segments. Do your customers want a particular experience from your retail channel? Do they expect quick simple service?*

Finding the correct channel of operation will be achieved over time and most retailers will adopt a number of channel options – multi-channel. Successful retailers are now embracing all channels and a mix of online and offline is by far the most successful model in the current retail market.[12]

[12]Join in Twitter conversations about Retail - All subjects are listed at the end of the chapter.

Summary

■ *Find your niche in the market for your customer segments*

■ *Develop your brand and brand values*

■ *Develop the brand 'voice' and 'imagery'*

■ *Decide on your channels of operation*

 Join in the conversations about Retail on Twitter by using:

Your brand is the identity of your business and your products, and often includes physical words, colours and logos #retailinspector [11]

A mix of online and offline is by far the most successful model in the current retail market #retailinspector [12]

3 | Establish your brand and niche

The Retail Handbook

11
Etail and
Social
Media

1
Know
your
customer

2
Know
your
product

10
Build
foundation
for growth

CHAPTER FOUR

**Build a
team to
compete**

3
Establish
your brand
and niche

9
Manage your
information and
finances

5
Market
your product
and brand

8
Merchandise
and manage
your stock

7
Customer
service is
everything

6
Launch the
business and
Sell, Sell
Sell

The
Retail
Handbook

Helping you achieve your **Potential** in **Retail**

4 | **Build a team to compete**

Building a high-performing team that acts as one and grows your business is the key to providing your customers with the best experience your business can possibly provide. Each person in your team has a role, which is extremely important to the achievement of satisfaction for your customers. All your team members need to know their purpose in your team and how that helps achieve customer satisfaction. The first area to develop is a customer-focused culture.

Develop a customer-focused culture

Culture underpins the entire business and helps your team understand how to act and behave when they are part of your business.[13] Culture looks at the values the business wishes to stand for, and is closely related to your brand, your product and your niche. Defining your culture is the place where the journey begins.

Defining the culture of a new business is hard to achieve, but the up-front time spent on developing this culture will be worth the time and energy. Understanding an existing culture is also difficult, but you already have a culture in place – you may just not realise that it is there and what it means.

Focusing completely on the customer segments you have defined and understanding your niche will underpin the process to define your culture.

[13] Join in Twitter conversations about Retail - All subjects are listed at the end of the chapter.

47

Once you have defined your culture, you need to implement practical plans to instil this in your teams, and make it become a way of life in your business – a way of operating that everybody naturally adheres to and one which represents your business in the way you would like it represented.

To develop a customer-focused culture you need to follow a structured process:

1. *Set aside at least one full day with your main team to brainstorm and discuss the culture you wish to develop in your business.*

2. *If you already have a retail unit, try and be in this space where the customers interact with your business – maybe a stock room or an office nearby. The purpose of this is to understand what the customer feels, and experience what they experience when they are interacting with your business.*

3. *Use the first part of the day to brainstorm all your ideas and views of the culture – these could be images, words, statements, sentences etc. – anything that will help you visualise the culture of the business.*

4. *Write and draw all these on flip-charts or post-it notes – discuss the ideas with your team to get more ideas flowing (at this stage no idea is removed and nobody makes a bad suggestion – everything should be written down).*

5. *Once you have all your ideas you can then start to formulate themes: What are the common images? The common words? The common sentences?*

6. *Pull together the themes on one or two flip-charts.*

7. *After a break from the brainstorming, return to the charts and use them to write the most important three as values – these are statements as to how you will operate as a business and how all your team will act.*

Please see the Culture and Values Development Case Study for a practical example of this process in the last part of this handbook.

It is important to spend time on this process, really invest the time to get underneath the real feelings and values that you have for the business and what the customers will want to see in every part of your business.

Recruit a high-performing team

Once you have a defined set of values and an understanding of the structure of your business, you can start to develop and recruit a team.

The starting point of the journey is a defined set of roles. Based on the structure of your business, whose aim is to service the customer segments, define each of the roles you need in your business. A job description is the obvious starting point and a standard job description can be used for all roles.

All the roles should be part of a structure that fits the business needs and services the customer.

An example hierarchy

In the example hierarchy we have a store manager at the top of the business; their role is to manage and lead the team to achieve the objectives of the business.

I would suggest three further areas:

▼ **Customer Service** – *These are the customer-facing teams, such as the sales assistants and customer support*

▼ **Stock and Finance** – *Combining stock with the finance team is important to ensure that you manage your stock well and maintain a good cash flow within the business*

▼ **HR/Training** – *This is an important role that helps manage the people efficiently (e.g. with staff rotas) and also ensures your teams are well trained and motivated*

This is a generic structure and you will have more or fewer people than this; the point to understand here is that a clear structure and hierarchy helps focus all your team on the end goal which is to satisfy and serve your customers.

Once you have completed a job description for each role, this can then be translated into a job advert for you to start the recruitment process. For the recruitment process, you also need to define the type of people you wish to employ, as well as the skills needed for the particular role. Understanding and defining the skills needed for a role is relatively simple, but what you also need is a 'type' of person that will be able to perform the role and be part of your customer-focused culture. If a person has the basic skills, you can train them to do the job that they are employed to do, but you cannot change a person's attitude and personality. This is how the person is internally and relates to their personal values – if they do not have similar values to those you want in the business, you will find there will be problems at a later stage in your journey.

A clearly-defined recruitment process is important and should involve finding out about a person's values, as well as their skills for the role. Knowing the values of your company helps you advertise the roles to recruit the 'right' type of person for your company. A great example would be looking at the local adverts for jobs in magazines or trade journals and see how the different companies write the different job adverts. For the same role, for example a store manager position, you will see completely different headlines and wording even though the role is in essence the same – the difference is the values and culture of the individual business.

A clear and structured interview process is important. Not only is this important for being professional and efficient, a structured and process-driven interview procedure will allow all members of your team to take part in the recruitment process, and ensure that you recruit your people fairly and as consistently as possible.

To recruit a high-performing team you need to:

▼ *Define the structure of the business, with the customer at the heart of the business*

▼ *Clearly define the roles, their purpose and how they link to your customers*

Practical Example

▽ *Define the 'type' of personality you are looking for in your team members. This will come from the values of the business that you have established*

▽ *Write the recruitment advert to appeal to the type of person that you would like to represent your company to your customers*

▽ *Hold a structured interview process that allows all members of your team to take part and have a consistent view of the potential team members*

Live and breathe values

The ultimate aim of developing the values is to have a number of statements that encapsulate all the thinking and planning for the values.

Case Study

How to develop values

Developing the values is part of the process to visualise and develop the culture. This will involve brainstorming to come up with ideas, words, sentences etc.

Once you have completed the brainstorm you then need to form these into sentences and explanations such as:

Provide World-Class Customer Service - "We will provide a World-Class Service to our most important Customer - your customer."

High Performance - "We will provide a High Performance environment where we welcome change and invest time and energy in developing our people."

Each of these is then broken down into bullet points of actions and behaviours that help you achieve these values.

Once you have developed your values and culture, you need to ensure this is set into the business from Day One and is a part of everything you and your team do.

The most important way to help the values to 'live and breathe' is to live them yourself; if you have developed the values correctly, you will already be an ambassador for these values, and will be living and breathing them naturally.

The following areas will help you, in practical ways, embed the values and help the business live and breathe them.

The Retail Handbook

Train the team

Training should start on Day One, and in a high-performing business will continue training forever.[14] The first day of a new team member's career with you should start with a basic introduction to the company: the products, the team and, most importantly, an introduction to who your customers are and how they should interact with them.

An important session for all your team members will be a 'culture training' session. This should happen in the first few weeks and take the new team members through the company values and explain what they mean and how they are applied in your business. The Culture and Values Development Case Study talks you through a practical example of a culture training session.

Training needs to become an embedded way of life, and your team members should want to continually develop themselves; if they develop themselves, then your company will also develop. Offering training programmes is a great way to build a team spirit and also help improve the overall competence within the business.

A way to find out what training a person needs, and keep them striving for high performance would be via a PDR process. A Performance Development Review process is where you appraise your team member's performance on a regular basis (maybe every six months).

This serves many purposes:

▼ *Review the past six months' performance*

▼ *Set objectives for the next six months*

▼ *Review training and development opportunities*

▼ *Receive feedback as a team member's manager*

To develop a high-performing team you need to:

▼ *Hold a short induction on Day One for all new team members – cover the basics of the business, the 'domestics' (where the toilets are, when the breaks are etc.), the health and safety rules and introduce the customer segments to the new team members*

▼ *Set the new team members a first few weeks' training and induction programme to ensure they have all the necessary connections and training they need to perform a great job*

---

[14] Join in Twitter conversations about Retail - All subjects are listed at the end of the chapter.

▼ *Hold a culture training session with every team member in the first few weeks – make sure they understand your company's values and how they should embrace these values*

▼ *Set up a continual performance development process – every six months review the performance of your team and set new objectives and training plans*

Communicate with the team

Communication with the whole team is important – from communicating the vision, to communicating the daily sales and trading performance. In general, every person in the business should be fully up-to-speed with what is happening and how these issues affect themselves, and more importantly, your customers.

Communication starts with sharing the vision for the business at the outset – your team needs to know why you are in business and what you are trying to achieve. Understanding the vision enables every team member to understand what they are doing to help achieve this vision and how they can change things if they are not working towards this vision. Having a vision, and common goals, helps bring teams together and bridges gaps between team members who may not understand what the other team members' job roles are, and how they all interact to provide world-class customer service to your customers.

Your customers will see your brand through your teams, and everything that your teams say and do. Making sure your teams are 'on the same page' is part of your daily routine. Informing your teams how the business is performing on a daily basis, what is doing well and what is not doing well, is important to ensure everybody is focusing on the main issues that you wish to resolve and improve.

Implementing a great communication process will help your business achieve its goals:

▼ *Make communication a priority across the whole business*

▼ *Hold a weekly team meeting where you discuss the previous week's performance, the learnings from this, the next week's highlights and any other important issues for your business in that week*

▼ *Ensure the main points from the meeting are relayed to the whole team shortly after the meeting*

▼ *Send out a report or have a daily morning meeting to cover off any issues from the previous day and issues for the day ahead (for example, new products or promotions that may be happening). Keeping these meetings to five minutes a day maximum is more than enough*

Develop loyalty in the team

Developing loyalty in the team will help keep the customers happy and satisfied – motivated and loyal team members will always give better customer service and be happy to go the extra mile for the customers. Loyal team members build consistency in the business and this helps to grow and develop the business for the customers.

Loyalty in the team helps to build rapport with the customers – when a customer sees the same person each time they visit your store, they feel more comfortable and are much more likely to shop with you again. This also significantly benefits the business, by allowing the team members to build up rapport with the customers who will then be able to gain more customer insights and more information about the customers' wants, needs and desires, allowing you to serve the customers better.

Loyalty is gained from working with the team and understanding the team. Setting up a strong culture and set of values, as described earlier, will help to make the team feel part of the business and help them live and breathe the values.

Loyalty from your team can be developed by:

▼ *Regular and informative updates (weekly/daily meetings)*

▼ *A good induction process, so they feel part of the business from the first day*

▼ *Regular performance and development reviews – keeping them on track and developing*

▼ *Incentives and rewards – offer discounts, product trials and benefits for achieving targets*

Create interest in your product and brand

Allowing and encouraging the team to interact with the products will grow loyalty and also allow for better selling of your products or service. If you have a team that knows and loves your products inside out, they are more likely to recommend the products sincerely to your customers – thus improving your sales.

Creating interest and excitement around the product is easy to implement at any stage of the product life cycle. During the planning phase you can use the team members as part of focus groups to discuss and debate the concepts and ideas you have for the current or new range. This can be very exciting for the team and make them feel fully part of the journey.

Once the product is launched you can allow the team to trial and test the product – taking the product home overnight, wearing the product or tasting the products are all easy to do and relatively inexpensive.

Discussing with the team the brand values and the products allows them to absorb the culture and start to become ambassadors for your brand – they will live and breathe the brand which will be seen by the customers and the people the team interacts with. This improves the selling ability of the team and makes it easier to interact with the customers.

You also need to ensure that during the trials, tests and focus groups, the team is finding out what the USP of your product is. Educating the team on why the product is different and what the benefits are for the customer will strengthen the selling ability of the team.

Creating interest in the brand and products can be achieved by:

▼ *Focus group and design team meetings*

▼ *Product testing – at home, trials, testing etc.*

▼ *Training the team on the benefits and USP of the products*

▼ *Allowing the team to live and breathe the brand*

Remunerate the team to perform

Remuneration is often seen as the most important motivator to people in the workplace. Setting the correct pay and benefits level is a pre-requisite for a successful and happy team. Money on its own is not a motivator or de-motivator – it is a factor that is expected and as such you need to manage this carefully. We all want to earn more money, but we also know the value that is placed on the job roles we fulfil. Pay and benefits need to be in line with the values of the business – a high-end retailer must remunerate the staff according to the high expectations and perceptions of the customer segments.

Money is the basic level of remuneration and is expected by all employees. Where you can be creative and motivational is with the benefits and incentives. These include many areas such as: bonus, holidays, discounts, pensions, car benefits, health insurance, training, etc.

Making these attractive and competitive is important. You do not want to over-pay or be driving up salary inflation. A real problem we faced in the Shared Service Centre (SSC) in Czech Republic was our ability to pay more; we could have started a salary increase across the whole region if we had set our salaries over the odds. Instead we offered better training and social activities to compete with the existing companies in the area, without increasing costs for the whole sector in the region.

Case Study

What is the SSC?

Providing good customer service is critical to successfully operating a business as large and complex as a multi-national retailer. As part of its drive to improve customer satisfaction, the business created an SSC for the finance function. The SSC was set up to provide financial services across several European countries and was located in Brno, Czech Republic. It had to service other companies within the group, across Europe, and had to provide the same customer service expected from its own retail stores. The Culture and Values Development Case Study has in-depth coverage of this topic.

The total rewards package needs to be flexible to allow all members of the team to feel motivated and appreciated. This can be measured and offered to all the team so they can choose what suits their life. For example, some people may like extra holidays, whereas others may like a higher pension contribution or bigger staff discounts.

Case Study

A great way to motivate and reward the team is via social events. This can be offering the team a budget to hold an event every month, holding a company Christmas party, subsidising a weekend trip or holding a summer BBQ and Olympics. This not only rewards the team, but it also builds team camaraderie and bonding.

A good remuneration policy motivates and rewards the team:

▽ *Benchmark the industry to ensure that you are competitive – look at outside companies or look at local jobs that are similar*

▽ *Offer flexible benefits – let the employees choose what they would like to take advantage of; for example offer extra training or hold social events*

▽ *Focus on non-cash incentives and rewards*

▽ *Use your products to provide benefits to both your team and your business*

Remuneration benchmarking within your industry can be completed in a number of ways, with the starting place being:

▽ *Local recruitment companies who deal with your local job market*

▽ *Your local government job centre will have information on local salaries and benefits*

▽ *Business support companies, such as your local Business Link and your local Chamber of Commerce*

▽ *Your local newspapers – have a look through the job adverts and you will get a great feel for the local salary and benefits offered by your competitors*

For more detail on developing a team to compete, please refer to the Culture and Values Development Case Study, which discusses in depth how to set up a culture and develop a highly motivated team. It discusses in detail the steps taken and the secrets to creating one of Europe's best customer-focused SSCs.

The Retail Handbook

Summary

- *Develop a world-class customer-focused culture, throughout your entire business*
- *Recruit a high-performing team*
- *Live and breathe your values and culture*
- *Train the team to compete and be the best*
- *Communicate with the team*
- *Develop loyalty in the team*
- *Create interest in your product and brand*
- *Remunerate the team to perform*

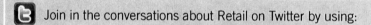 Join in the conversations about Retail on Twitter by using:

Culture underpins the entire business and helps your team understand how to act and behave when they are in your business #retailinspector [13]

Training should start on Day One, and in a high-performing business will continue training forever #retailinspector [14]

4 **Build a team to compete**

1
Know your customer

2
Know your product

3
Establish your brand and niche

4
Build a team to compete

6
Launch the business and Sell, Sell Sell

7
Customer service is everything

8
Merchandise and manage your stock

9
Manage your information and finances

10
Build foundation for growth

11
Etail and Social Media

CHAPTER FIVE

Market your product and brand

The
Retail
Handbook

Helping you achieve your **Potential** in **Retail**

5 | Market your product and **your brand**

Having set up a great business with an amazing product range, a clearly-segmented customer base and a great team to deliver this, you need to then move into marketing your product and your brand. Marketing is the means by which you inform people that you and your products exist and takes many forms.

Marketing is often seen as advertising alone, through media such as TV adverts, newspaper adverts and online adverts, but marketing is much wider than this. Marketing looks at many different channels and forms, which all inform the customer that you and your products exist.

Forms of marketing

Advertising

Advertising is the first area that people consider when they talk about marketing. An advert is paid for and appears at exactly the time and place you want it to. You control its contents and its placement. The main advertising media are:

- ▼ *Newspapers*
- ▼ *TV*
- ▼ *Radio*
- ▼ *Magazines*
- ▼ *Online (e.g. banner adverts)*
- ▼ *Online paid marketing (e.g. Google Adwords and Facebook adverts)*
- ▼ *Outdoor*

The basic requirements for any advert

An advert can appear in a number of media as mentioned above, but must fulfil a number of basic criteria.

A good advertising campaign and theme will include:

▼ *A clear message* – *an advertising campaign must have a purpose and this purpose should be clear and consistent; this is known as a 'call to action'. For example, a retailer will give the message that you need to visit the store to see the new range or buy the latest offers in store*

▼ *A theme* – *a clear and coordinated theme is important, keeping all wording, imagery, messages and goals the same and for these to be seen as the same no matter what media channel is used*

▼ *Easy to understand* – *every advert must be simple and easy to understand. Each day we are bombarded with adverts and brand messages; to compete, yours must be simple and easy to understand in a few seconds*

▼ *Eye-catching* – *similar to the above point, we are all time-pressured and we need to see and understand the advert in a few seconds*

▼ *Coordinated and consistent* – *across all the types of media and the media channels, the messages and themes must be consistent for the customers to understand*

▼ *Call to action* – *the advert must have a call to action – i.e. there must be a call for the reader to do something; that could be visit the physical store, call a telephone number, visit the E-commerce website or watch a certain TV show*

▼ *Brand driven* – *overall the brand values must be seen in the advertising. Adverts are normally the first contact a new customer will have with your business, so the adverts must portray the brand image that you have developed for your business*

▼ *A strapline* – *a common sentence that spans all the media and becomes well recognised. Large retailers use this extremely well – for example 'Every Little Helps' and 'I'm Lovin' It' are well-known straplines that we see on all their adverts, be that TV, press or online. Not all companies use this, but it can be used to expand the brand understanding*

A good marketing strategy will involve a comprehensive marketing campaign – this is where you co-ordinate a number of adverts, in a number of media and marketing channels. These must all 'feel' the same to the customers. Each separate type of media must portray the same message and image as the others; you should make sure that you develop a comprehensive theme that can span all the types of media and channels you wish to use.

How we created a strapline and adverts for FreshMax Shirts

The brand strapline took a few weeks to develop. We had to be very careful about mentioning 'sweat' as this is a personal and emotional word, but the benefit of our shirts was that you did not show sweat patches and therefore the shirt was great for all men – and we needed to tell them this.

The discussion always led us to the benefits being 'improved confidence'; if you have sweat patches, you notice it and you are aware of it. This makes you less comfortable and in turn less confident.

We eventually decided on the strapline:
'Show nothing but confidence'

This encapsulated all we wanted to say about the benefits of the shirt; it was our strapline at launch and still is to this day.

We also developed a sentence that described the shirts – we had to say what they were so that the customers could understand the product.

We used: **'The only shirt that eliminates sweat patches'.**

This strong sentence was important to explain what a FreshMax Shirt was and why you should buy it – it describes our USP.

Other forms of marketing

Advertising is the main form of marketing; other forms of marketing are discussed later, and include PR and sponsorship.

Tell the customer what you sell

In its most basic form, marketing is about telling the customer what you sell and why you exist. [15] Marketing your product should ensure that the customer is aware that you exist and understands what products you sell – the aim of marketing should be to ensure that when people hear your brand they recognise that you sell a certain product range.

Over time, with brand marketing, you will expect the customers to be able to understand not only what you sell, but also know what your brand stands for and what they can expect when they shop with your business, i.e. they begin to understand your culture and your values.

When you are marketing to your customer, keep it simple; make sure they know what you are selling, at what price (if this is part of the marketing message), where they can buy the product and why they should buy your product from your retail channels.

Making the customers aware of your products must be simple and efficient – a customer sees hundreds of marketing message each day, so a succinct and easy to remember marketing message is the key to success.

Tell the customer what the benefits of your product are

Once you have told your customer what you sell, you need to sell the benefits of your product versus your competition. You have already defined your customer segment and established what your customers want from your products; you now need to ensure that the customer knows what the benefits of your products and services are.

This is easy to forget and take for granted, but customers will not know what your product benefits are unless you tell them – building a brand and a business takes time, and you will always need to remind your customers what are the benefits of shopping with you.

Making the customer aware of your niche and your USP is key in your marketing messages – you have built your product and service for your customer segments and now you need to make sure they are aware of what you have developed for them, and how this satisfies their wants, needs and desires.

[15] Join in Twitter conversations about Retail - All subjects are listed at the end of the chapter.

To make sure your customers know about your products' and services' benefits you must:

▼ *Communicate the benefits to them, clearly and consistently*

▼ *Make sure the communication is simple, but comprehensive*

▼ *Make sure you know your customers' communication preferences – find out what is their preferred method. Ask them via questionnaires, VIP events, asking your team etc.*

▼ *Communicate in the ways that they like to receive information e.g. mailings, emails, Tweets, telephone calls etc.*

Case Study

How did we develop the adverts at FreshMax?

The adverts had to centre on sweat, but not the negative images of sweat; we needed 'confident and free' images and statements.

We used two of our brand images of the customers and made two separate adverts based on improving your confidence:

1. Meeting the Board? No Sweat – A confident man with his arms back looking like he is the most confident person in the board room:

2.   First date nerves? No Sweat – A very happy young man with his arm around a beautiful girl, looking and feeling very happy, without any sweat patches:

The adverts had a theme that highlighted an occasion when you would feel nervous and start to sweat more than normal, and ended with 'No Sweat' as this was what the shirt provided the customer. A great benefit of 'No Sweat' was that its second meaning is to relax and take it easy – this was exactly how our customers wanted to feel in a stressful situation.

Develop a promotional strategy

Initially your marketing strategy will involve your product and is very likely to talk about some type of promotional offer or event. It is important to develop a promotional strategy as early as possible and make sure this strategy is achievable.

A good promotional strategy will focus on the customer and what they will value the most in a promotion – some customer segments will value money off, others link-buys (to sell two products from different ranges that complement each other, such as a DVD player and a new release DVD) and others a VIP or exclusive event. Work with the customer segments and the brand values you have established and develop the promotional strategy to achieve these objectives.

A promotional strategy should cover:

▽ *The types of promotions relevant to your customer segment*

▽ *Enhance and add value to any marketing campaign you are running*

▽ *Be of greater perceived value than the actual cost e.g. a VIP event is perceived by customers of greater value than the actual cost of the event, or a free product with a purchase will be calculated at cost price and therefore be part of the whole strategic cost and benefits of a marketing campaign*

▽ *Set up the strategy at the beginning – you may decide to hold promotions at regular intervals or as and when you have good offers and product deals*

'Two track' marketing

In retail we talk about 'two track' marketing, which are two very separate marketing processes that have two different objectives: Brand Marketing and Product Marketing.

1. *Brand Marketing is when you market your brand and your values, rather than a specific product or group of products. This is normally a long-term programme and the results will only be realised in the longer period of time as people become aware of your brand and what your brand represents to your customer.*

2. *Product Marketing is when you market a specific product, products or product range. This is the main marketing that retailers use and what you will see the majority of the time in adverts and promotions.*

In this chapter, we will talk, in the main, about product marketing as this delivers the sales results you need to keep the business trading day to day;

brand marketing is a longer-burn process that you will do as part of an overall marketing strategy. Assuming you have the product marketing plans in place and working first, you can then press ahead with your brand marketing alongside product marketing to help drive more understanding of your brand and awareness of your products.

Marketing channels

There are two main marketing channels – Online and Offline – both of these we will look at separately, but they should be used together, not separately. Understanding how your customer interacts with your business will help you choose the correct channel, and trialling different channels is a great way to find the perfect fit for your product and service.

Online marketing involves marketing your products and services in the intangible world of the internet, mobile phones, smartphones and using social media.

Please see the online retail chapter for a greater understanding of the differing online marketing channels. In summary, the main areas are:

- ▼ **SEO (Search Engine Optimisation)** – *Ensuring that your website is well-ranked in the search engines, i.e. when you type your product or service into Google you want to be one of the first companies in the list offering the product, so new customers can visit your website*

- ▼ **Affiliates** – *This is where you allow another website to market your product to their customers in return for a commission*

- ▼ **PPC (Pay Per Click)** – *This is advertising on the search engines (like Google) and paying every time a person clicks on your links*

- ▼ **Direct Adverts** – *Setting up an advert directly on a website and paying for the placement of this advert*

- ▼ **Social Media** – *This is using the social media sites to make people aware of you and your product, and in some cases directly advertising*

- ▼ **Blogs** – *Blogging is writing something related to your company and posting online to create interest and awareness of your brand and your products*

- ▼ **Articles** – *Writing articles on your subject of expertise and sending out on your website to build awareness and credibility*

Offline marketing has been used for a long time and is also known as traditional marketing. This type of marketing is much more tangible than online marketing, and has been tried and tested over the years. Offline marketing is used less than it was a few years ago, but it is nevertheless a very important channel.

The main types of offline media:

▼ *TV*

▼ *Radio*

▼ *Magazines*

▼ *Newspapers*

▼ *Journals*

▼ *Catalogues*

▼ *Samples*

▼ *Events*

▼ *Posters*

▼ *Leaflets*

The main channels used for smaller retailers are normally newspapers, magazines, leaflets and local radio. Your choice of media should be dependant on what your customer segment uses. Understanding which media they use, and which media they value, will help you decide which form of media to use.

These types of media are more expensive than online and their results are much less measurable, but they are still the largest channels of media used, and customers still expect to buy your products after seeing adverts in these media channels. The number of types and the variety of these types means that there will be an excellent fit for your products and for your customers segments. Research, and some trial and error, will find which channels work the best for your business.

These channels have changed over time and will continue to change. Understanding the types of customers for each media channel is important, as these will have changed over the last few years and will change over the next few years as customers wish to interact with your business in different ways.

Above all, the main goal is to make sure your advertising campaigns are co-ordinated and cross all the media channels your customers use, both online and offline.

Sponsorship, community and events

These media channels are often very beneficial to market a business or product. They can also provide something back to the community, as well as raise awareness of your business inside the community.

Sponsorship of a local group, be that the local youth football team or the local community group helping people back into work, can be used to help promote your brand and products, but also help you become part of your community.

Businesses that are seen to be helping and developing the local community will benefit from an improved image and brand perception. You can also use this connection to train and develop your teams – team building at the local school by painting the building, or helping out at the local old people's home, are fun ways to build a team and gain valuable PR and news coverage.

Involvement in the community can also involve offering your expertise, product and teams to help improve parts of a community in need of your skills. Again, this will allow you to develop a reputation within the community and grow an awareness of your brand.

If you operate nationally rather than locally (i.e. on the internet) you can still sponsor other websites and charities; for example you could sponsor a national bike race or national 'get fit' week. The cost of the sponsorship should be seen as part of the marketing cost for your business and decisions will need to be made as to what events to support.

When your scale allows, you can grow into sponsoring TV shows and national events such as football tournaments or other major events.

Being a part of the community is an important part of marketing and growing your brand awareness. Look at the opportunities you have in your area and try out a few ideas – volunteering your and your staff's time once a year will cost very little, but could return a whole new awareness of your business and your brand.

Components of a marketing plan

To market your brand successfully you need to set up, from the outset, a marketing plan that will cover all the areas we talk about in this chapter. A marketing plan covers all areas of marketing and is mainly external-looking, whereas the marketing strategy looks at what you need to achieve and what you need to implement for a successful marketing function.

A plan should be developed in detail and shared by the whole team, so that all areas of your business know what the plan is and what the desired sales and customer service targets are.

A marketing plan should encompass an in-depth review of the following areas and help lead to the marketing strategy document that is the summary of the plan and, more importantly, the focus for the marketing goals and targets for the business.

▼ *Market Summary* – *A number of statements discussing the market as a whole and where you sit within the market. It will build on your plans for your niche market and your understanding of your customer segments*

▼ *Market Demographics* – *This is the vision and view of your customer segments and their lifestyle and values*

▼ *Market Segmentation* - *This is the summarised understanding of your customers and the customer segments you are targeting*

▼ *Market Positioning* – *This summarises where you would like to position yourself in the market. It follows on from the niche and brand building plans you have completed*

▼ *Market Needs* – *Understanding what your customers, and therefore what the market, demand from your products and your services*

▼ *Market Trends* –*The important trends that shape the niche market you are in and direct the current and future plans for your customer segments*

▼ **Market Growth** – *Being able to understand the physical current size of your market and the forecasted growth of your niche in this market*

▼ **SWOT Analysis**

Strengths – *The internal strengths of your business and proposition*

Weaknesses – *The internal weaknesses within your business*

Opportunities – *The external opportunities to improve and add value to your business*

Threats – *the external threats to your business*

▼ **Product Offering** – *Your product range and your USP*

▼ **Keys to Success/Critical Success Factors** – *These are the important elements you must have within your business and factors that you must take into account to be successful*

A Marketing Strategy Template

A good marketing strategy covers a number of areas; it starts from the mission of your business and ends with measurement of the results.

An important point to note here is the statement: 'What gets measured gets managed'. This will help ensure you achieve the target and mission of your business by measuring the outcome of the plans and strategies.

This strategy will pull together work that you have done in the previous chapters, and is a great place to start to summarise the business strategy for a perfect focus on marketing, which in turn will lead to sales and profits.

In the table over I introduce the section of the strategy and give you the FreshMax examples to help bring this alive for when you complete this exercise.

SECTION	FRESHMAX ONLINE EXAMPLE
The mission of your business	Sell FreshMax Shirts online and commercially prove the technology and the fabric
Customer segments and sources of growth	Men, South East, 20-45, ABC1
Competitors	Shirt retailers and sports technology products
Differentiation (your USP)	A shirt that eliminates sweat patches and looks and feels like any other high-quality 100% cotton shirt
Strategies and action plans	See Case Study
Measurement of the results and financial plans	See Case Study

The mission of your business

The mission is a statement of why you exist and what you wish to achieve. Specifically, what your company wants to achieve is the goal. This could also be called 'a statement of ambition' for your business.

The process of developing the mission has been started in the previous chapters, where you have looked at your customer segments and your target markets. You can now pull this together and ask yourself: "How should we position ourselves in the marketplace to secure long-term success? What type of retail offer will we provide?" etc.

Spending time answering these questions will help to develop your mission which forms the top of the marketing strategy, i.e. the main goal for your business.

Customer segments and sources of growth

We have spent a chapter discussing and developing your customer segments, and we have talked about how to define your market; here is the place to summarise and review your thinking and planning. This part of the strategy is to clearly define who you want to sell to, and how you will generate growth for these segments. Both of these areas are critical for the development of the marketing strategy.

Customer segmentation will help you understand who you are targeting, and how you will talk to them[16]– define a particular customer segment in the marketplace that will be your audience for your products. Once you know your customer segment, you need to know exactly who you are targeting with your marketing, how you will talk to them and in what voice.

This involves defining the forms of marketing media you will use and how you will develop a full marketing campaign.

5 | Market your product and your brand

Further breakdown on the FreshMax customer

The FreshMax customer was defined as:

- ▼ *Men*
- ▼ *A,B,C1*
- ▼ *20-45*
- ▼ *Living in London/South East*
- ▼ *Full-time employment*

Their lifestyle:

- ▼ *Urban professionals*
- ▼ *Like/need to look good*
- ▼ *Internet savvy*

We targeted men only because the product launched initially would only be men's shirts and we chose London and especially Canary Wharf because:

- ▼ *London's business centre is now Canary Wharf*
- ▼ *The most densely populated area of the country*
- ▼ *Over 1.24 million people, either working or shopping*
- ▼ *75% aged 25-44*
- ▼ *The highest earnings per head of anywhere in the country - over £100K pa*
- ▼ *A captive audience who work, shop, eat and drink in the Wharf*

Competitors

In every retail market there will be a number of competitors offering the same or similar products; understanding who these are and what they offer is very important.

You must review all your competitors and focus on the key competitors; who are the most important ones you will have to compete against? There will be a small number of your competitors that you will need to focus on, and you will need to develop a strategy that will enable you to compete successfully with them.

Differentiation (Your USP)

When you developed your market niche and brand you also developed your USP – here you can use that analysis to answer the question: What will make you different and attractive to your customer segments?

This is a review of your previous work, putting this into a number of clear points of differentiation that you can talk about in your marketing strategies.

Strategies and action plans

Once you know your mission, your customers and what you offer that is different, you can then develop strategies and priorities that will achieve these plans.

Ask yourself what you need to do and how, in order to deliver on this strategy. What resources will you require? What systems? How will the plans be executed? etc.

Put together a number of priorities. These will form the everyday work of the entire business – if you are doing something that is not one of your priorities, you should not be doing that task.

Measurement of results and financial plans

Developing a marketing strategy with clearly-defined targets and goals will help you achieve the overall mission of your business. Setting the goals is the first step of the process; the final step is to measure the success of the achievements.

When you initially set your strategy, ask yourself: "What will success look like? What investment will be required and what return will be generated?"

Answers to these questions can then be measured and monitored, to ensure you are on track.

The importance of marketing

Developing a marketing plan and strategy is a long process that builds upon your understanding of your customers and your products. It is a great model to use, to pull together all your previous planning and thinking about your customer, your niche and your product range.

A marketing strategy that has clear targets and measures is the main goal for the marketing part of your journey.

Putting together the marketing strategy, with your mission and goals, allows you to develop a plan that can be implemented via the marketing channels we discussed at the beginning of the chapter.

This plan should be shared with all your team so they can understand what your business will be doing to market the right products to your customers.

 Join in the conversations about Retail on Twitter by using:

In its most basic form, marketing is about telling the customer what you sell and why you exist #retailinspector [15]

Customer segmentation will help you understand who you are targeting, and how you will talk to them #retailinspector [16]

5 Market your product and your brand

Summary

- *Understand the main forms of marketing*
- *Develop the basic requirements for an advert*
- *Tell the customer what you sell*
- *Tell the customer what the benefits of your product are – your USP*
- *Develop a promotional strategy*
- *Understand 'two track' marketing – to build the brand and to sell products*
- *Know the different marketing channels available to you Sponsorship, community and events*
- *The components of a marketing plan should be followed*
- *Implement a marketing strategy*

5 | **Market your product and your brand**

1 Know your customer

2 Know your product

3 Establish your brand and niche

4 Build a team to compete

5 Market your product and brand

6 CHAPTER SIX
Launch the business and Sell, Sell, Sell

7 Customer service is everything

8 Merchandise and manage your stock

9 Manage your information and finances

10 Build foundation for growth

11 Etail and Social Media

The **Retail** Handbook

Helping you achieve your **Potential** in **Retail**

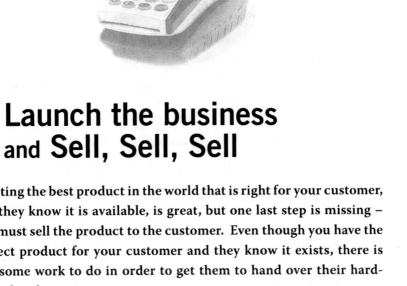

6 | Launch the business and Sell, Sell, Sell

Creating the best product in the world that is right for your customer, and they know it is available, is great, but one last step is missing – you must sell the product to the customer. Even though you have the perfect product for your customer and they know it exists, there is still some work to do in order to get them to hand over their hard-earned cash.

Selling is informing the customers about the benefits of your product[17]

When a customer decides to buy a product, they have a need, desire or want they seek to fulfil. For example: When a customer decides to purchase a drill, they do not want to buy the drill; they want to hang a shelf on the wall, and therefore need to make a hole in the wall. Or a customer buys a pair of Armani jeans, not to keep warm but to express their fashion image and their personal status.

Understanding the benefits of your products means understanding what is important to your customer and the reason why they would enter your shop or visit your website. They visit your stores because they want a product that fulfils a need, desire or want they have.[18]

Inform customers about the product benefits

[17-18]Join in Twitter conversations about Retail - All subjects are listed at the end of the chapter.

Selling is enabling the customer to buy your product

Selling is the final stage to enabling the customer to buy your product at the right price, right time and with the right quality. Selling involves focusing on the benefits of your product – telling the customer why they should buy your product.

You already know what the customer wants and you know what they value and like in life, you have set out your brand image and implemented a quality level – you must now sell your product to your customer.

Enabling the customer to buy the product involves informing them the:

▼ *Product exists (via marketing)*

▼ *Product is available to take home or for delivery*

▼ *Benefits of the product (its USP)*

▼ *Pricing structure of the product range*

▼ *Added extras of the product (service plans, VIP clubs, link-buys etc.)*

Selling techniques

There are many selling techniques that are available for retailers and many different proven strategies. Here I will discuss the basic process and the simplest form of selling a product to a retail customer – this is mainly focused on a customer who is in a physical shop, but the principles can be adapted for an online store.

The basic principle in any selling transaction is to understand that the process is two-way – the customer has a need, want or desire and you have a product that meets that need, want or desire. Your team's role is to match the two in a simple and pleasant way, thus making the customer happy and making your business happy. This is called a 'Win-Win' scenario – when both parties are happy with the result and leave your business feeling satisfied.

The aim of the dialogue is to find out why the customer is in your retail outlet or has visited your website – what is their need, desire or want?

The two-way process in action:

▼ *The first piece of information you need from the customer is why they are in your store – you can ask many questions to open this dialogue. Questions such as "Good Morning/Afternoon/Evening, What brings you into our store today?" This is an open question that allows the customer to discuss with you straight away the problem or reason why they need your product or service*

▼ *Finding out why they are in your store allows you to work out which benefits of your product will appeal to them and answer their question of what problem they are trying to solve with your product*

▼ *There are many reasons why customers visit your store, and capturing these trends over time and for each of your customer segments will be very useful to train and develop your team, and also to plan further marketing and further growth strategies*

▼ *Once the customer is engaged, make sure you 'close the sale'; you must ensure you actually ask the person to buy the product and get them to pay or order the item. This is as easy as saying "You can pay for this over here" or "Would you like this gift-wrapped?"*

▼ *Do not be afraid to close the sale – selling products is why you have the retail business in the first place*

▼ *Do not be afraid to up-sell and cross-sell. Up-selling is a process where you sell a higher value product to a customer based on the additional benefits the product offers and the needs of the customer*

▼ *Cross-selling is offering a complementary product that is beneficial for the customer to purchase. For example, when you buy a DVD player you normally need a cable to attach it to your TV – without this, the DVD player is useless and the customer will be disappointed*

Selling online is slightly different, as you cannot engage in a direct two-way conversation as easily as you can within a physical store. An online sale is focused on the planning beforehand and understanding the needs of the customer before they visit your website. You then need to make sure your website easily answers the needs of your customers. Making your website simple and direct will mean the customer can find the product and buy it with ease.

Setting up a clearly-defined online product catalogue is important to enable the customer to find the products they need, based on their reason for visiting your store. Over time you can adapt the website to answer questions for the customers, for example: 'Having problems putting up your shelf? Click here to see our latest range of drills'.

Using social media can help an E-commerce website sell the benefits via the different means available[19] (for more detail on social media see the etail chapter).

Using a checkout that is simple and intuitive is important to close the sale. A one-page or integrated checkout is the most successful, which allows quick access of details and the ability to check out in one click.

At the checkout you can also cross-sell and up-sell. Analysing your customers' purchases will allow you to link products that you know customers will see as complementary to their purchase or needed with their purchase.

Make sure the sales process is in line with your brand values

Understanding your customer segments and their values is very useful for developing your selling process. You must ensure that your sales process reflects the values of the brand and that of your customers. You should not over-sell your products, and neither should you under-sell your products – both of these will cause customer service issues and complaints.

We have all experienced the hardcore selling tactics – known historically in the car sales industry, where it was common for them to use any tactics possible to get you to buy a used car. This approach is still used in some high-pressure sales channels, but in the main these are not common in retailers and in most cases would cause a negative result from the customer.

[19]Join in Twitter conversations about Retail - All subjects are listed at the end of the chapter.

The selling process should be in line with your values and cover:

▼ *An understanding of how your customer likes to shop and therefore how they would like to be treated when they interact with your business. A high fashion store will have a very attentive service and sales process, whereas a local newsagent will be a quick and pleasant interaction*

▼ *Acknowledging the customers, and making sure they know that you and your team are there for them, is important for all sales opportunities – make sure you greet all your customers and apply the right amount of sales pressure your team feels necessary in order to fulfil the customer's need, and gain the important closed sale*

Launching your business
– new, refreshed or a new product range

When you set up the business, renew or refresh the business or develop a new product range, you need to plan a launch campaign and PR plan, to capitalise on the opportunity to gain 'free PR' and make sure you get off to the best start you possibly can.

PR (Public Relations) is very different from advertising and is the process by which you approach the press (TV, radio, newspapers, magazines, bloggers, articles etc.) to write an article about your new product or store.

Good PR is being able to deliver an interesting story to the readers of the media[20] – all journalists need interesting stories to engage their readers on a regular basis, so any great news story is beneficial to them and their readers.

It is important to make sure there is a story – opening a new store or launching a new product range is an OK story, but it needs some interest and relevance to the receivers of the press.

Delivering interesting stories to the readers of the media is always good PR

[20]Join in Twitter conversations about Retail - All subjects are listed at the end of the chapter.

Thinking about the details of the story is important and could be, for example:

▼ *A local focus: 'Local store opens and employs 10 people from the local community'*

▼ *A new and interesting focus: 'Retailer launches brand new shirts that eliminate sweat patches'*

▼ *A good news story: 'Retailer launches new product range that is 50% less wasteful'*

Developing an interesting story is a simple process:

▼ *Draft a few 'news' stories about the launch*

▼ *Review the PR channels and target the ones that suit your launch campaign*

▼ *Tailor the articles for the relevant readers/consumers of the articles – make it relevant to the end readers*

▼ *Write the article and make it easy for the journalist to use and understand – they have very little time and many articles to read each day*

▼ *Develop a plan and co-ordinate the whole process. Be aware that PR is not controlled and you can only give the best shot at getting into the relevant press you would like it in*

▼ *Collate all the PR and use that in your adverts – PR builds credibility and is important for brand building*

The final part of the launch is to hold some form of launch event – making sure that a large number of people know you have launched is very important to give your business the best start possible. Plan an event and invite the relevant people, e.g. a local store opening: invite the local dignitaries, the local press and some of the local community; for a new E-commerce website, launch on the relevant blogs and news spaces, as well as social media platforms.

The most successful PR campaign is planned and thought out – some of the PR will not be used or not work, but you must plan a number of different PR items and a few of them will give you the desired effect.

A real example of a well-executed PR plan was at FreshMax. When we launched the E-commerce website in July 2009, we managed to have a spot on GMTV the launch week, followed by the BBC the following month and a few months later a full Reuters network story and interview.

We worked with our PR partner, advertising partner and creative partner to agree a plan to launch the product in July 2010.

The plan was based on two stories:

1. The product technology itself and what the benefits of the world's first shirt to eliminate sweat patches would be.

2. The development story of two young English guys who spent eight years developing the technology.

The plan was set up to send the PR introduction sheets to the press, magazines, TV, bloggers etc. and then follow up with meetings and product samples.

The PR campaign was a massive success, and on the day of launch the inventors appeared on ITV1 with an interview and a full two-minute test of the product. In the video, the ITV presenter wore the shirt on a bike and in a sauna, proving the technology worked. This was the perfect start to the business launch and helped prove that the shirts really do exist and they do stop sweat patches showing – even in a sauna.

That was followed by the BBC Sunday morning show, discussing the product and again testing the product on the show. The press and magazines coverage then took hold of the story, and we were in most of the main newspapers and magazines during the first six months of launch.

By January 2011 we had PR coverage in all national UK newspapers, BBC and ITV1, Reuters news networks, a large number of magazines and international coverage including a Sunday newspaper in Australia and a fashion magazine in the USA.

The Online Retail Case Study explains in much greater depth the process we used to market and promote the FreshMax Shirts E-commerce business.

Launch the business and Sell, Sell, Sell

Summary

- *The selling process is informing the customers about the benefits (USP) of your product*
- *Selling is enabling the customer to buy your product*
- *Understand selling techniques*
- *Make sure the sales process is in line with your brand values*
- *PR - Launching your business (new, refreshed or a new product range)*

 Join in the conversations about Retail on Twitter by using:

Selling is informing the customers about the benefits of your product #retailinspector [17]

A product that fulfils a need, desire or want they have #retailinspector [18]

Using social media can help an E-commerce website sell the benefits via the different means available #retailinspector [19]

Good PR is being able to deliver an interesting story to the readers of the media #retailinspector [20]

6 | Launch the business
and Sell, Sell, Sell

11
Etail and
Social
Media

1
Know
your
customer

2
Know
your
product

10
Build
foundation
for growth

CHAPTER SEVEN

Customer service is everything

3
Establish
your brand
and niche

9
Manage your
information and
finances

4
Build a
team to
compete

8
Merchandise
and manage
your stock

6
Launch the
business and
Sell, Sell
Sell

5
Market
your product
and brand

The
Retail
Handbook

Helping you achieve your **Potential** in **Retail**

7 | Customer service is everything

Welcome to the customer service chapter; this is only a small chapter as the whole book centres around the customer. This chapter looks at specific customer service best practice that is not part of the other steps in the journey.

Customers are the key to the success of your business; without them you do not exist and without them you cannot be successful.[21] Making the customer the heart of your business is the only way to achieve retail excellence. The positive effect of a total customer focus is a happy customer, which in turn makes your teams happy, which makes you happy and also makes your business profitable in the process.

Think Customer – everybody is a customer

Every part of the business must Think Customer[22] – you only exist to service the customer and therefore every part of the business must understand how their actions affect the ultimate customer. Thinking Customer involves immersing the whole business in your customer's lifestyle and how your customer likes to live and shop.

A world-class customer service culture is developed by ensuring all the team understand not only how they affect the end customer, but how they are also a customer and everybody they interact with is part of the customer's journey.

[21-22]Join in Twitter conversations about Retail - All subjects are listed at the end of the chapter.

Every team in your business has a customer and is a customer; a customer in this case can be described as anybody you interact with in your daily routine. The easiest way to think of this is to look at, and treat, everybody you interact with as if they were the ultimate end customer who buys your products. Greet them, chat with them, understand them and then deliver what they need from you. This is applicable to everybody in the business, no matter what their responsibilities are.

A great example of this is when I set up the Finance Shared Service Centre (SSC) in the Czech Republic, and I instilled a culture of customer service. The fact that the work performed at the SSC was totally removed from the ultimate customer was irrelevant. Some of the team were processing invoices for the retail business; these team members are very unlikely to ever meet the ultimate customer, but their role is so important.

I use an example to explain this: If the team member does not process the invoice correctly, a supplier does not get paid. If this is escalated and again another team member does not react correctly, the supplier will be out of pocket. If this continued to happen, the supplier will stop sending their products to the retail stores and ultimately there will be no stock to sell to the customers and the business will go bankrupt.

This example is extreme, but it highlights the important role everybody has to play in order to service the ultimate customer, and ensure that they all play their part in the team and meet their responsibilities.

Trained and customer-focused teams

A happy, trained and motivated team will always offer the best customer service they possibly can – they are trained and motivated to do so. Training your team starts at the interview, where you must ensure you recruit customer-minded and customer-focused team members. Once you have recruited these you must train them on who the customers are and what they value.

Valued team members not only provide good customer service, but they also motivate each other to keep themselves improving and delivering for your business. We have talked about how to recruit, train and develop a team in earlier chapters and the Culture and Values Development Case Study.

Keep the customers loyal

Once you have established a relationship with your customer you must maintain this relationship. A loyal customer is of great value to your business, because they know you, like you and shop with you. When you have loyal customers you can easily email or call them with your latest offers or new product ranges, to enable more sales and gain more information about your customers.

Loyal customers are also the best sales team you will ever have – a happy loyal customer will tell all their friends about your products[23], and their personal recommendation is not only free, but also means more to the potential customer than any advertising and marketing campaigns that you may run.

For an online business the loyal customer is even more important due to the use of social media – imagine your customer 'Tweeting' about your great store experience or the great product they have just bought – this can be read by millions of people and help drive traffic to your website and customers visiting your physical store.

To keep a loyal customer you need to give them what they require from your business; you will know this from understanding your customer and developing your products for them. You need to be consistent in your execution within your business and ensure happy customers leave your business every time.

Making your customers feel special can be achieved by:

▼ *Regular updates on what's hot and what's new*

▼ *Interesting stories about the business and the team*

▼ *Regular incentives and special offers*

▼ *VIP events and offers*

▼ *Talking to them and listening to their feedback*

Simple returns and exchanges

This area of customer service is easy to forget during the journey, but is and area that must be made simple and efficient – especially with an online store. Customers expect to have the ability to change their mind and change their products, as easily and simply as possible. Poor returns

---

[23]Join in Twitter conversations about Retail - All subjects are listed at the end of the chapter.

and exchanges will prevent customers from shopping with you in the first place. In the current retail world, the customers' expectation is that they are able to exchange a product if they do not like it – a no quibble and no fuss exchange or return.

A good returns and exchanges process involves implementing:

▼ *A clear returns and exchanges policy stating how long the customers have to return the items, what condition, where to send them, etc.*

▼ *Trained teams that know how to deal with the returns and exchanges – make sure all your team know how the returns and exchanges process works to ensure great customer service*

▼ *A process for disposing of product or reselling the returned product*

▼ *A way for the customers to send the products back easily – free returns labels and some companies are now offering a returns service from a local 'drop shop'*

Test the customer service

A well-trained, customer-service-focused team will be able to service your customers every day in a consistent and positive way, but sometimes team members' attention will slip, and you need to ensure that consistency is applied all the time.

Using test shoppers and mystery shoppers is a big benefit to any serious retailer; all the large retailers carry out regular tests and mystery shops to ensure the processes and training procedures are correct, and work for the customers.

When you carry out a test or mystery shop, ensure all the feedback is captured, and feed back this experience to the team members involved, to help improve their own way of working. You can also use the total data to address any company training issues or process issues that may have been exposed.

Customer feedback is key to your future success

Gathering as much customer feedback and opinions as possible will help you grow and develop your business successfully. Keeping close to your customers enables you to find out what works, what does not work and what needs to change.

Implemented in a positive way, customer feedback can drive your future growth and planning decisions, as the customer can tell you what they want from your brand and your business.

Using all the possible channels to gather this data is important and you should utilise as many as possible:

▽ *Email data*

▽ *Your teams' interactions*

▽ *Questionnaires*

▽ *Sales data*

▽ *VIP events*

▽ *Surveys*

▽ *Blogs and social media monitoring*

▽ *Incentives and promotional events*

Gathering this data will help you throughout the journey and is mentioned in most sections of this handbook – it is an important part of understanding your customer.

Think world-class customer service

A total understanding of your customer is the best way to achieve your potential in retail.[24]

How do you develop a total understanding of your customers?

▽ *Develop a total customer-focused culture*

▽ *Remember: Everybody you and your teams interact with is a customer*

▽ *Train your teams on customer service and customer interactions*

▽ *Inform your teams of the different customer segments you target, why you target these and what they 'look' like*

▽ *Focus your teams on interacting with the customers, let the teams spend time with the customers so they can be your 'eyes and ears' on behalf of the customers*

▽ *Keep your customers happy and loyal – a loyal customer is a 'free' sales channel*

▽ *Test the customer experience*

▽ *Gain as much customer feedback as you can – this can help you develop more and more profitable sales, products and ranges*

[24]Join in Twitter conversations about Retail - All subjects are listed at the end of the chapter.

Summary

- *Think Customer – Everybody is a customer*
- *Develop trained and customer-focused teams*
- *Keep the customers loyal*
- *Simple returns and exchanges*
- *Test the customer service*
- *Customer feedback is key to your future success*
- *Think world-class customer service*

 Join in the conversations about Retail on Twitter by using:

Customers are key to the success of your business; without them you do not exist and without them you cannot be successful #retailinspector [21]

Every part of the business must Think Customer #retailinspector [22]

Loyal customers are the best sales team you will ever have – a happy loyal customer will tell all their friends about you #retailinspector [23]

A total understanding of your customer is the best way to achieve your potential in retail #retailinspector [24]

7 Customer service is everything

7 Customer service is everything

96

11
Etail and
Social
Media

1
Know
your
customer

2
Know
your
product

10
Build
foundation
for growth

CHAPTER EIGHT

**Merchandise
and manage
your stock**

3
Establish
your brand
and niche

9
Manage your
information and
finances

4
Build a
team to
compete

7
Customer
service is
everything

6
Launch the
business and
Sell, Sell
Sell

5
Market
your product
and brand

The
Retail
Handbook

Helping you achieve your **Potential** in **Retail**

8 | **Merchandise** and **manage your stock**

Making sure your stock is correct for your target market helps you deliver world-class customer service – your customers are ultimately visiting your store to buy your stock. You need to ensure that everything is perfect, with the right stock, in the right place, at the right price for your customer segments that your business targets.

Stock is extremely valuable and should be viewed and treated as if it were cash.[25] Stock has two financial values: the first is the stock value which is the price for which you bought the stock; the second is the retail value which is the price for which you intend to sell the stock.

The difference between the two is the margin. This could be very large or small depending on whether you are in a high-value or low-value business. The size of the margin is linked to the way you manage your costs and will make you a profit or loss.

The right stock

Understanding what is the right stock, and sourcing this at the right price is key to being able to satisfy your customer needs. Your customer segments will inform you what your product range should be, and from that range you can decide what the exact product mix should look like. Research and test market all the variants possible: colours, sizes, styles, brands, options etc. and make sure the products are complementary to each other and fit well as a range in the customers' eyes.

Buying the right stock will come from your sourcing strategy and will be redefined at this stage as you begin to order and forecast what quantities you need to buy in order to meet the customer demand.

The best initial stock level

Deciding on the correct stock level at the beginning is difficult; you have no history and your products, service and brand combination is unique. Spending time planning the first orders is important, not only because it is a big cash investment, but also due to this being the first range and you need to ensure full availability during your opening period.

Understanding your customers' buying patterns will happen over the first few weeks, so your initial plan should be to satisfy a reasonable forecast of what you will sell before your second delivery of products will arrive. As part of your sourcing strategy you will have decided on the distribution plan and this will need to be tested during your first few trading weeks.

The best initial stock level means you need to forecast your sales until your second delivery and ensure you have enough stock for full availability during the initial days of trading.

Once you have been trading a few days, out of stocks are less important as you start to understand your customers' shopping patterns – it is important to keep the stock levels tight as you learn how your customers shop and in what quantities they buy your products.

You will over- or under-forecast some products and maybe even some ranges – this is to be expected. Nobody can ever forecast the exact requirements of the customers. Make sure you have put in place a process to deal with under- and over-stocks – under-stocks will need a good customer service response, e.g. "We can order the product" or "We have this product which is similar" and over-stocks must be dealt with quickly via markdowns and promotions.

Manage your continuing stock levels

Maintaining a good level of stock is a hard task to achieve in the first few months of trading. Stock management is affected by many outside influences that, in the main, you do not control. Knowing your optimum stock level for your business at the start is based on your best guess. The

8   Merchandise and manage your stock

more planning you have done and the more time you have spent with your customers and team, the more reliable your forecasts will be.

When you plan your sourcing strategy you will have looked at how you will distribute and warehouse your products. This plays a role in deciding on your continuing stock levels.

If you can negotiate more regular deliveries, you will need to hold less stock – thus being cheaper and easier to manage, but you may run out of stock more often, which could lead to poor customer service. You need to plan where you think your balance is between the two and refine it over time.

Forecasting the initial stock needs to be an educated guess using the facts and information you are currently aware of. You could use the following to build up your forecasts:

▽ *Any previous history*

▽ *Other shops'/businesses' data and trends – Use your networks and see the section 'You have more connections that you realise' in Chapter 2*

▽ *Data and forecasts from your suppliers*

▽ *Customer feedback*

▽ *Team feedback*

▽ *Sales plans you have in place*

▽ *Marketing, promotions and PR you are planning*

Develop a commercial/buying plan

All these forecasts should be used to start a commercial plan. A commercial or buying plan is a forecast of what you need to buy in order to fulfil your expected sales. You already have a marketing and promotional plan in place; a commercial plan should be implemented to ensure that you buy enough products to fulfil your sales and marketing plans.

Once you have a few weeks' sales history, you can set up your stock replenishment process. This is a process by which you re-order or review your stock levels when you are nearing the end of a product's current stock holding.

Feeding your sales data into your commercial planning process enables you to automate the process based on rules. For your main stock range you could set minimum levels at which you order stock.

For example, you may have a supply chain that takes four weeks from order and you know you sell 100 items a week. When you get to 450 items you should re-order; this is because you currently sell 100 items a week and delivery takes four weeks, hence you will have 50 items left when the new delivery arrives.

This process can be put in place for all your products at an individual product level, but should be reviewed often as sales patterns change.

Cost price negotiations

Agreeing a cost price on every product is a trade-off or balance between three competing areas:

▼ **Price**

> *The price you pay for the product*

▼ **Payment terms**

> *The agreed length of time you have to pay the supplier for your product*

▼ **Quantity**

> *The amount or level of stock you wish to buy*

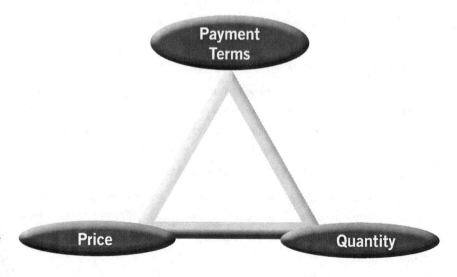

The balance to be achieved between these three areas depends on your own business's needs and resources:

▼ **Price**

> *Do you have the cash to invest in stock? A bank loan can be agreed and the stock used as a guarantee if needed*

▼ **Payment terms**

> *Can you afford to pay your suppliers sooner or later?*
> *You can always 'factor' these invoices – this means that a bank or finance company pays the supplier sooner rather than later and you pay them at a later date*

▼ **Quantity**

> *Do you have enough room to store a large amount of stock?*

The trade-off should look at how much you are willing to pay for a product and how long you wish the repayment period to be.

For example; I have a small stock room and a low cash holding. It would be best to negotiate a slightly higher cost price, but a longer payment period, to ensure I sold the products before I paid the supplier, but I also make a good gross profit.

Using a commercial plan and modelling tools, you can easily calculate the best cost price to agree, the payment period and quantity.

A shirt retailer is negotiating the purchase of a new range for the next season. The plan is to sell 500 shirts and the retail price will be £40.

The initial terms from the supplier are: £15 for 500 units (in one delivery) and 30 days to pay – therefore £7,500 is due in 30 days from delivery.

You have a look at your budget and realise that you only have £2,500 cash in 30 days, but will have £6,666 in 60 days as you will have sold 200 shirts (£33.33 retail price less 20% tax).

You therefore propose to the supplier that you commit to 500 units with payment terms of 60 days.

The supplier will want to increase the cost price for the longer payment terms and he may propose £16 per shirt.

You could then agree the deal and go ahead with your committed order.

How much to order - minimum order levels

A minimum order level and also a minimum order quantity should be calculated. Once your products reach the minimum stock level, you need to calculate how many to order – this can be a rule, based on stock levels required and warehousing capacity.

For example, you could re-order at 450 stock level and you re-order for four weeks (100 items sold per week), therefore ordering another 400 items.

Over time you can make many rules to calculate these figures to ensure you have the optimum stock level to meet the customers' needs and manage your cash and risk levels.

If you do not want to have this level of sophistication, you can buy on a regular basis, i.e. every month, and each time you order have a look at what you sold the previous period and what you forecast to sell in the next period. Make sure you include any promotions and marketing campaigns you may have planned.

The commercial planning process looks at the following areas:

▼ *An understanding of your product range*

▼ *A forecast (by individual product) of what you think you will sell in a set period of time*

▼ *An understanding of your marketing, PR, launch and promotional strategy will drive part of the forecast*

▼ *An understanding of the desired stock levels*

▼ *A re-order process to calculate how many to order and how often*

▼ *An understanding of sourcing and distribution*

▼ *A view of the markdown process*

▼ *A plan to remove poorly-performing stock*

Once you have the initial plan you can start to use this plan as a basis for the future. Add the actual sales figures to the forecast plan and start to track any trends that are appearing; these will help build you better forecasts in the future.

The main points to take into account in a commercial and buying strategy:

▼ ***Buy frequently*** *– negotiate a deal on long delivery products and 'call off' the stock at regular intervals*

▼ ***Manage the stock accurately and carry out stock takes regularly*** *– you need to know your stock is accurate so you can forecast future orders and fulfil your customers' needs*

▼ ***Act on slow sellers*** *– do not be afraid to mark down products as soon as you realise they are not selling – clearing out slow sellers not only frees up cash but allows you to replace the products with new products the customers want and desire*

▼ ***Check the commercial plans versus the marketing and promotional strategies*** *– does it look like you have enough stock to fulfil the plans? Are you buying the correct products for the plans and promotions?*

▼ ***Do not be over-optimistic*** *– we all like to be positive and bullish, but you must balance a big forecast and order against the stock not selling and you making a loss on all your products. It is better to sell out in the first few weeks rather than run out of cash and go bankrupt because you are not selling all the stock you bought*

Calling off stock

Calling off stock is a process by which you forecast your stock requirements over a long period (say one year), but only commit to the amounts you need nearer the time.

For example:

You 'commit' to buying 500 blouses for the next season – i.e. you reserve these blouses. The season's launch is in three months' time, and you will need delivery four weeks in advance. You move from a 'commitment to buy' to a specific order of, say, 250 blouses to be delivered in eight weeks' time.

Once you start selling these, or you know you will be promoting these strongly, you 'call off' some more stock, knowing that you still have another 250 blouses reserved for you.

This gives you an advantage of a good price for the large volume order, but manages your risk if things do not sell as well as you thought in the beginning.

It also enables you to buy the best and most relevant stock for your customers and keeps the lead times low.

Stock is Cash

Cash is the most important financial measure in a business; businesses fail due to lack of cash, not due to lack of profits.[26] After fixed assets such as the building and fixtures, stock is likely to be the biggest investment a retailer makes and, ongoing, one of the biggest costs in the business. Planning your stock is critical to the company's financial health and a wrong decision could ultimately bankrupt the retailer.

Managing the buying price (the price you pay for your products) is important to make sure you will make a profit, but you also need to manage the stock turns (the number of times you sell the products each year) and the stock holding. Both factors affect cash and product availability, and ultimately will affect the customers' experience.

A faster stock turn with more frequent deliveries is the best option – this frees up cash and deals with poorly-performing products quickly. New ranges appear often and the customers are kept excited and enticed by your constantly-changing product range that is targeted to them.

You will often have a large proportion of core products that you always sell, and a smaller proportion of new and exciting stock that you buy in smaller quantities and sell to your loyal customers.

Good stock management involves:

▼ *Good commercial plans that are linked to the marketing plans and based on sound financial forecasts*

▼ *A defined product range*

▼ *A good supply chain and warehousing strategy*

▼ *Thorough checks of the delivery quantities*

▼ *Regular and thorough stock checks*

▼ *Quick action on poor sellers and markdowns*

▼ *Fast stock turns*

[26]Join in Twitter conversations about Retail - All subjects are listed at the end of the chapter.

▼ *Exciting new products*

▼ *Management of theft and loss – all retailers suffer from products going missing*

▼ *Management shrinkage – all retailers suffer from products being damaged*

▼ *Good returns and exchanges management*

▼ *Special care of high value stock*

Develop a markdown strategy

A markdown strategy is a plan of how you will deal with stock that is not selling as well as you had planned. All ranges will have some products that do not meet the customers' needs and will not sell as well as the rest of the range. You must act on these products quickly – remember that stock is cash and stock not selling is destroying the value of that cash.

To develop a markdown strategy you need to go back to the values of the brand and define what types of markdowns and promotions you wish to operate.

There are many options available but you would normally use:

▼ *Percentage reduction*

▼ *Fixed reduction*

▼ *Buy One Get One Free*

▼ *Multi buys e.g. 3 for 2 or buy this product and get another half price*

▼ *Money off a following visit or purchase*

Setting a formal markdown process is important to manage profits, minimise losses and keep the stock moving. An example of a markdown strategy for a fashion store: one month after launch of the range, products that have more than 75% of the average stock level for that range should be discounted 10%, one month later that should be 20% etc.

Developing a markdown strategy from the beginning of your journey will enable you to clearly implement the rules of markdowns as part of your normal operating business.

Reviewing your stock levels and your markdown discounts should be fully calculated and some products you will sell at a loss. This is normal practice in retail; the key is to make sure you sell more products at a higher margin and profit than you sell at a loss.

Merchandise to sell

Buying the right stock for your brand and image needs to be thought of when you plan the merchandising of your range. Merchandising describes the methods you use which contribute to the sale of your products. In a physical store, merchandising refers to the product range available and the display of your products in such a way that it stimulates interest and entices customers to buy your products. The same rules apply online – setting out your homepage and catalogue structure is important to understand for good customer service.

When you plan your range, you must think about how the products will look to the customer,[27] and how easily the customer will be able to find the products they need. Arranging your product range is very important; your customers need to be able to find easily what products you sell and identify where the products are located in the store or online.

The main element to merchandising is the way you display and position your products. Making your products look the best they possibly can and be as 'in situ' as possible is important. Making your products look 'in situ' is achieved by setting up a store that is similar to where the product will be used by your customers.

For example, in fashion stores the use of mannequins is the main way of displaying products in situ, and in a cooking products store laying out products on tables etc. will help the customer find the products they wish to purchase.

You can use merchandising principles to differentiate to your customer segments. We all know fashion stores are split ladies' and men's sections, and then casual and formal, but you could also set up 'lifestyle' sections (use the imagery from your customer segmentation process) and you could then set up a mannequin that is dressed in a total 'lifestyle' look, e.g. sporty or dinner date etc. Merchandising all the products physically nearby will help the customer imagine what it would look and feel like to own all your product range.

[27] Join in Twitter conversations about Retail - All subjects are listed at the end of the chapter.

Merchandising accessories and linked products near to your core products is very important. For a linked or secondary product, you must make it simple for the customer to buy the product. Retailers normally do this in one of two ways:

▼ *Put the secondary products by the core merchandise, e.g. belts near trousers, batteries near toys, cables near DVD players*

▼ *Put the secondary products by the tills – this is very common in supermarkets*

On the E-commerce store you can easily purchase programmes that show related or linked products when the customer adds products to the basket or when they are checking out.

Segment your product range for the customers

Segmentation should be customer-focused, not your own internal buying plans. This is very important and a very common trap that retailers fall into; for buying and merchandising purposes it is easier to follow your product development plan and therefore be internal looking. If you have followed this book and set your product range up for the customer segments, you will already be able to merchandise for the customers.

A great example of non-customer-focused segmentation is in the electricals retailing industry. The standard names for the categories are: brown, white and grey goods – what are they? As a customer, do you know (or care) what a white good is? The truth is you do care, as you want to buy a washing machine; you just need to know which area the product is in. You would find a washing machine in the kitchen appliances section. In a customer's view (in store and online) these will be categorised as: TVs, Computing, Large Appliances, and Kitchen Appliances etc. – categories that a customer understands and would look for in a shop.

Summary

- *Find the right stock and the best initial stock level*
- *Develop a commercial/buying plan*
- *Manage your continuing stock levels*
- *Cost price negotiations*
- *Stock is Cash*
- *Develop a markdown strategy*
- *Merchandise to sell*
- *Segment your product range for the customers*

 Join in the conversations about Retail on Twitter by using:

Stock is extremely valuable and should be viewed and treated as if it were cash #retailinspector [25]

Cash is the most important financial measure in a business; businesses fail due to lack of cash, not due to lack of profits #retailinspector [26]

When you plan your range, you must think about how the products will look to the customer #retailinspector [27]

8 Merchandise and manage your stock

8 | Merchandise and manage your stock

11
Etail and
Social
Media

1
Know
your
customer

2
Know
your
product

10
Build
foundation
for growth

CHAPTER NINE

**Manage your
information
and finances**

3
Establish
your brand
and niche

8
Merchandise
and manage
your stock

4
Build a
team to
compete

7
Customer
service is
everything

6
Launch the
business and
Sell, Sell
Sell

5
Market
your product
and brand

The
Retail
Handbook

Helping you achieve your **Potential** in **Retail**

9 | Manage your information and **finances**

Once your business is up and running, you will have vast amounts of information which is very valuable to your business, if you manage it correctly. Using real data that is from the trading of the business and from your customers can help improve and develop many parts of your business.

Understanding your finances and managing them is key to a successful and profitable business.[28] Knowing where your money comes from and goes to is something you should understand on a regular basis – even daily for sales and cash. Remember: you must manage cash correctly – Cash is King and without cash your business will fail.

Know and understand your Profit and Loss account

Your Profit and Loss account (P&L) is the place to find out where your money comes from and where it goes to. It starts with the money coming in (Sales Revenue), it takes off the cost of those sales (Cost of Goods Sold) to give you the profit from your product buying (Gross Margin). Once you have your gross margin you take off all your other costs and you are left with your profit (or loss).

P&Ls should be reviewed on a weekly or monthly basis – in the beginning, managing your P&L daily is important to make sure you know where you are spending your cash. Understanding the P&L allows you to make business decisions based on real facts within your business. Over

[28] Join in Twitter conversations about Retail - All subjects are listed at the end of the chapter.

113

time you will need to make positive and negative decisions, and these will all have an effect on the P&L; understanding that impact before you make a decision is very important.

The easiest way to get to know your P&L is by looking at it regularly; starting with sales which you can review every day.

Plan, Forecast and Budget your finances

It is important to start planning what the costs and revenue impacts are to your business of all the previous plans that you have been developing on this journey. Once you have an understanding of your product, commercial plan and an understanding of your marketing and sales plan, you can then put together a budget or forecast that predicts what you plan to sell each week and what the cost of those sales will be.

With the rest of the plans you have looked at, you will then be able to forecast the costs within the business. These can then be measured to ensure you are on track and the business is performing as you wish it to.

A basic P&L format (this can be Budget, Forecast or Actual) is below.

Budget/Forecast/Actual	Period 1	Period 2	Period 3
Sales Revenue			
Cost of Goods			
Gross Margin			
Costs:			
Staff			
Rent/Rates			
Marketing/Advertising			
Store Overheads			
Delivery/Logistics			
Finance/Admin			
Profit before Tax			

This format can be used for different periods (i.e. weeks, months, years) and different types (i.e. Actual, Budget, Forecast). All formats should remain consistent and all items should be calculated in the same way; this will enable comparisons and trends to be analysed.

Cash is King

The management of cash will make or break a business – businesses fail due to lack of cash, not lack of profits;[29] therefore managing the cash and the bank account is extremely important.

The retail industry is a great 'cash' industry that most industries would be jealous of, due to its ability to manage to a positive cash flow situation. This means that as a retailer (in certain sectors) you can retail products that are bought by the customer before you have paid the supplier – this is called positive cash flow, as you will have the money in the bank from the customer before you pay for the products you just sold. Since the financial crisis this has been much harder to achieve, but striving to achieve a positive cash flow is a great target.

The way to manage to a positive cash flow situation is to set up your suppliers' payment terms for a longer period than you need to sell the item; for example, if you negotiate payment terms of 60 days with your supplier and you sell the product to your customer for cash on Day 30, you will have 30 days left before you pay your supplier. Of course, to make this happen you need to have a trading history, a good credit record and be able to sell the majority of your stock sooner than you pay the supplier.

Whichever method you use to manage your supplier relationships and customer relationships, you need to manage cash on a daily basis. A simple reconciliation each day of your sales revenues and your costs can easily ensure you know where you are with your finances.

[29] Join in Twitter conversations about Retail - All subjects are listed at the end of the chapter.

115

An example cash flow statement is below.

Budget/Forecast/Actual	Period 1	Period 2	Period 3
Balance Brought Forward	£5,000	£10,000	£8,000
Sales Revenue (Cleared)	£10,000	£10,000	£10,000
Cost of Goods		£10,000	
Costs:			
Staff		£2,000	
Rent/Rates	£5,000		
Marketing/Advertising			£5,000
Store Overheads			
Delivery/Logistics			£2,000
Finance/Admin			
Balance Carried Forward	£10,000	£8,000	£11,000

In this example cash flow, we started the period with £5,000 in cash in the bank and made cash sales of £10,000. We then paid the rent and ended the period at £10,000 cash in the bank. This was then rolled forward to the next period and we then spent £2,000 on staff expenses leaving £8,000 in the bank.

As you can see, this simple model will ensure you can monitor and manage your cash – at the end of any period you should be able to reconcile the Balance carried forward figure easily to your bank balance and any borrowings you may have.

Planning your cash flow from Day One will help you understand your peaks and troughs with regard to cash. Most retailers have seasonal peaks and, in the main, this happens at Christmas (for example an electrical retailer will make 60% of their profit and sales in the three months from November to January). Managing cash during the quiet periods could be challenging, as there will be times of the year when sales are very low, but you still have to pay monthly bills etc. Planning this in advance will allow you to approach your bank and ask for a flexible loan or an overdraft – most retailers will use flexible financing through the quieter sales periods.

Customers and debtors

A debtor is an entity that owes your business money for services or products and in the main they will be your customers.

Managing customer payments into the business depends on the type of product you offer and can involve:

▼ *Cash*

▼ *Credit cards*

▼ *Invoicing*

▼ *Payment plans (i.e. Hire Purchase agreements or store cards)*

▼ *Deposits*

▼ *Loans over a long term*

The aim of the best cash flow policy is to get the cash as quickly as possible into your business, and the obvious quickest way to achieve that is to ask the customers to pay with cash. Unfortunately this is not a possibility in most retailers today.

Credit cards are the normal method of payment in most retailers now, and this will deposit the cash into your bank account in three to ten working days. Most people expect this instantly, but this is not the case and you need to manage the payment terms to reflect the number of days before the real cash clears your bank account as cash.

Invoicing is used for larger orders and more business-related sales; this is where you invoice the customer on the day of purchase and allow them

15, 30 or more days to pay. With invoicing it is important to manage the debtors (the business or person that owes you the money) and make sure that you chase the invoices if they have not been paid on time. It is also worth credit checking the customers and setting each customer a credit limit, so that you manage the risk of any bad debt and non-payment of your invoices.

If you offer instalments, again you need a strong process to manage the payments and ensure that you receive all the payments due to you, and on time. Longer term loans and credit agreements can be outsourced to a financing company, which will take the risk away from your business and take a small commission for their risk and taking on the debt.

Suppliers and creditors

A creditor is an entity to which you owe money – the main creditor to a retailer will be your suppliers, but you will also owe money to a number of other parties, such as landlords, service providers and the tax man.

Managing your suppliers is an important part of managing your profitability and your cash flow. When you are negotiating the buying price for the product you must also agree the payment terms; in cash flow terms, the longer the payment terms the better, but there is a balance between a good product cost and a good payment term.

Using the cash flow planner and making sure you know when your customers' cash clears will help you decide what the best payment term plan is for your business and what plan you need to agree with your suppliers.

In summary, to manage your cash efficiently you need to:

▼ *Plan and forecast the cash flow*

▼ *Negotiate payment terms with your suppliers*

▼ *Ensure you collect the cash from your customers*

▼ *Consider staggered payments both into and out of your business*

▼ *Negotiate flexible financing with your banks*

Analysis identifies trends and aids good decision making with regards to your cash flow and finances.

Analyse your information

Analysis is best described as 'making sense of information and data'. In your business you will have a lot of information and data – from sales, customers, products, adverts etc. and all this data is useful to you and your business. As long as you can understand what the data is telling you, you will be able to act on this information.

Finding out what all the information and data means is where you start to do analysis. Analysis needs to be simple and customer-focused; you are looking for trends and information that will improve your business,[30] which means the improvements you need to make to enable your customer to be satisfied.

The main analysis any retailer will look at will be the sales and the margins. You need to understand what this is telling you: where you are selling products, what products are selling and what products are not selling. You also need to understand what products are making you a good margin and what are making poor margins, and act on this analysis.

A list of the main areas to analyse is below (this is just a start; in your business there will be many more things that you can analyse to help improve your business):

▼ **Sales**

What products are selling

What products are not selling

How many products are selling

What customer segments are buying

Which channels are products selling in

What times of the day and which days do products sell

▼ **Margins**

What each product margin is

How much you are marking down/discounting products

Which customer segments are better margin contributors

▼ **Costs**

Staffing

Logistics and Delivery

Marketing

Promotions

Overheads

---

[30] Join in Twitter conversations about Retail - All subjects are listed at the end of the chapter.

Analysis of all these areas will help to identify trends and these are important for decision making. For example, if you analyse sales by customer segment, you may find that one segment is continually buying lower margin products; you can then investigate why this is happening and work out a strategy to convert these customers to higher margin products.

Once you have identified a trend, and you have investigated the reasons for that trend, you must act and develop a strategy to improve or develop this trend. Ongoing analysis and building up an understanding of the trends and drivers within your business will help you buy better products, reduce costs and make a healthy profit.

Lots of information and analysis is great, but you need to act on this information and make sure you put plans in place to achieve the improvements desired. Many businesses make the mistake of not acting on the analysis and end up in a worse situation because of this – make sure you make a decision and change things based on the analysis.

Information is Power

The more information you have in your business, the more likely you will be able to make sound decisions, based on good analysis and trends. Examples to collect as much information as possible have been shown all the way through your journey and keeping collecting data is a good practice to get into.

Once you have all the information for your analysis, as described earlier, you can then make informed and sound decisions to develop and improve your strategy. Collecting raw data from your sales and systems is a great process to implement, but you also need to collect customer data and more subjective data – this is the data that comes from your teams and customers, via everyday interactions, events and questionnaires.

Building up a stronger picture and understanding of your customer will allow you to buy better products and market your business better to achieve the customer satisfaction of your customers' wants, needs and desires.

Managing the information in your businesses requires specialist skills, which you may need to outsource or recruit these skills into the business. Recruit for or focus the analyst on:

▼ *Understanding and analysing the raw sales and financial data*

▼ *Establishing trends in the figures*

▼ *Cross-referencing and sense-checking the data. Does it look reasonable? Is it telling us some useful information?*

▼ *Understand the information deeper – data will show trends that happen, but you need to understand why this is happening. You do this by looking at customer data and feedback, discussing with your teams and asking the relevant people their opinions and views*

▼ *Use the information to make decisions – make sure the information and analysis is robust enough to enable you to make decisions and plan new strategies*

Find a good accountant and tax advisor

Finding a good accountant that understands you, your business and your industry is important. This will help you manage your finances in a successful way, and make the most of all the opportunities your business will have. Your accountant should understand your business and the goals and strategies of your business, to ensure that the advice they give and the support they provide is aligned to your goals and ambitions. There is no point employing an accountant that is focusing on cost management, when you know that you need to focus on how to improve the sales revenue or how to develop better gross margins.

Discussing your long-term plans with them will allow them to plan the best financing and tax structures for your business. There are many different funding options for your business and some will be leveraged to great advantage in your particular business. Knowing these different options, which are unique to the way you operate your business, will help achieve the goals you are aiming for.

Tax and corporate structures need to be developed to support you at the beginning and as you grow. The ultimate goal and structure of your business can be defined and driven by an efficient structure from Day One.

A good accountant should provide:

▼ *A thorough understanding of your current business finances*

▼ *Display an awareness, and interest in, your future plans*

▼ *Be able to use your cash flow to good effect*

▼ *Structure your company for now and for your future plans*

▼ *Input their view on your strategies and plans and provide ideas and resources to support these*

Ultimately a good accountant can be worth their weight in gold; you need to find one that understands your business and make them an integral part of your team. This will help get the best out of them now and in the future.

 Join in the conversations about Retail on Twitter by using:

Understanding your finances and managing them is key to a successful and profitable business #retailinspector [28]

The management of cash will make or break a business – businesses fail due to lack of cash, not lack of profits #retailinspector [29]

Analysis needs to be simple and customer-focused; you are looking for trends and information that will improve your business #retailinspector [30]

9 Manage your information and finances

Summary

- *Know and understand your Profit and Loss account*
- *Plan, Forecast and Budget your finances*
- *Cash is King*
- *Manage your customers and debtors*
- *Manage your supplier and creditors*
- *Analyse your information*
- *Information is Power*
- *Find a good accountant and tax advisor*

9 Manage your information
and finances

The Retail Handbook

11 Etail and Social Media

1 Know your customer

2 Know your product

9 Manage your information and finances

CHAPTER TEN

Build a strong foundation for growth

3 Establish your brand and niche

8 Merchandise and manage your stock

4 Build a team to compete

7 Customer service is everything

6 Launch the business and Sell, Sell Sell

5 Market your product and brand

The **Retail** Handbook

Helping you achieve your **Potential** in **Retail**

10 | **Build a strong foundation** for **growth**

Setting up any business or growing a business is extremely challenging in any market. Retail is a massively competitive market, but is full of many opportunities that have been missed by the larger retailers[31] or missed by the current smaller retailer base.

A new retailer, or an existing retailer wishing to improve their business, should focus on the customer and making sure they achieve what the customer wants; if they do that they will be successful. In order to build a sustainable and successful business longer term, you must build a strong foundation for the future potential of your business.

Ensure everything you set up and put in place is capable of supporting your business in the long term as you grow and develop.

Make your foundations strong

We all know that the best-built houses are built with very deep and strong foundations – the type of houses that were built hundreds of years ago and are still as strong today. It is hard to build a strong foundation, because it feels like you are digging down and not achieving anything, but this is exactly how successful retailers operate. They spend more time analysing, planning and building than they do operating; once they start daily operations, the team and the business runs itself (with a trained team in place) and the owners can focus on building the next set of strategies because they know the foundations are in place to support this growth.

[31] Join in Twitter conversations about Retail - All subjects are listed at the end of the chapter.

Building a strong foundation is part of building a brand and developing that brand. Once you have created a brand, you need to live and breathe that brand in all you do and make sure it is growing every day. Building a brand and an identity will allow you to get better at all you do, and allow you to become known for success and great customer service.

Spending time on building a strong foundation and culture allows a large and successful business to be built and developed.

Network and build connections

Networking and building your connections is a very important skill to master when you are in business.[32] Having a strong network of partners, suppliers and customers that understand your business and can support your business will help you grow and achieve your potential.

There are many different types of networks, the main ones I use are listed here:

▼ *Business networking (e.g. business breakfast networks)*

▼ *Business events (e.g. local library training)*

▼ *Free training (e.g. PR courses)*

▼ *Free events (e.g. speaking events)*

▼ *Clubs (e.g. members' clubs of fellow business people)*

▼ *Business set-up training (e.g. new business programme training days)*

▼ *Government/Not for Profit bodies (e.g. Business Link, UKTI)*

▼ *Social media such as Linkedin and Facebook*

A number of these companies want to do business with you, and offer free events for your attendance where you may learn from the training or the speakers, but you will also benefit from meeting the new people and connections that will be at the event.

Most people want to invest and help other businesses, and people like to be surrounded by successful people. Make sure you attend network building events – you never know who knows who, and what you will benefit from attending such events.

---

[32] Join in Twitter conversations about Retail - All subjects are listed at the end of the chapter.

Make yourself 'searchable' and connectable
– use social media:

Make sure that your website, Linkedin, Facebook and Twitter accounts are up to date and ensure you are near the top in any search list.

Here we have a Google search on my name and the first connection is to my Linkedin profile:

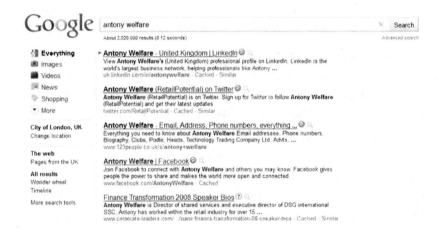

The Linkedin profile is then full of information about my career, recommendations and details that would interest any possible business partner.

Making yourself 'connectable' by using social media helps build credibility for you and your business – this opens the door to new opportunities and ensures you control the view of yourself online.

Mentors

The final area I will talk about on the subject of networking is mentoring. One of the most powerful influences on my business career has been the learning and support of my mentors. Over the years I have had many people who have advised and helped me with my businesses. Although I did not class them as mentors at the time, I now realise these people were mentoring me and advising me on my journey.

The most successful mentors have not been planned; they have been born out of a relationship with a business partner that helped me on my journey during that period of time. Some mentors will last for a long time, others will help you with smaller parts of the journey.

It is important to reflect on your own business support network – do you have many people that help and support you, do they challenge your ideas and advise you when things are challenging? If you do not have this yet, I suggest you start networking now – attend some of the events I have mentioned and make sure your social media presence is up to date and informative.

Understand what works and do more of it

Spend time understanding which parts of your business are working, which products sell the best, and which marketing strategies are the most successful – then do more of these.

Any business that knows what works for them should implement more of those actions; it will grow and develop the business, and if it is currently successful, it will be making the customers happy.

The opposite side of this is to drop ideas and plans that do not work; this is often hard to implement. For example, you have spent a few months developing a new product range which turns out to sell very badly. You must drop the range and move on to developing another range that is better and more focused on the customers. Learn from the things that do not work, find out why they do not work and make sure you do not make the same mistakes again.

Focus on the things you are doing that work and that achieve your goals and meet your strategic plans – anything else should not be happening, as it will not help you longer term and will not be making your customers happy.

Review all parts of your business:

▼ *Analyse the information and data that exists in your business*

▼ *Ask the customers what is working and what is not working*

▼ *Find out from the team what is good and bad*

▼ *Develop the areas that work*

▼ *Drop the areas that do not work*

Utilise new technologies

The world is ever-changing with newer and faster technologies. Only a few years ago people mentioned the 'World wide web'; now we take it for granted, and most of us use it every day of our lives. The web has transformed business and will continue to develop in the future.

It is not just the internet that is changing business, but new technologies are appearing every day and it is your role to find out what these are, how they can improve your business, and how they help to improve your customers' lives. These could be technical innovations that you can retail or new ways of developing products that means they are cheaper, more ethical or better.

An open mindset is needed as part of your culture; all ideas should be embraced and analysed to see if they could work in your business.

Think outside the box and develop new and innovative solutions for your products and services[33] – new ideas and inventions often seem crazy at the start, but over time they become the norm.

To find out about new technologies, innovations and inventions:

▼ *Ask your customers what they are using now and what they want in the future*

▼ *Follow your industry news and see what is hot and new*

▼ *Watch your competition, have they worked out how to do things better, quicker, smarter?*

[33] Join in Twitter conversations about Retail - All subjects are listed at the end of the chapter.

▼ *Embrace the internet and online shopping*

▼ *Develop and grow your use, and understanding, of social media – this is a massive new area of growth that can transform companies in the future*

Grow with your customers

You have worked hard to gain your customers' trust and you must now keep them and develop with them. They will be growing in the world and experiencing new things, you must find out what these are and what they want from your business.

Find out how they want to shop with you, interact with you and feel about your brand. Don't be afraid to test new ideas with them: new products, concepts or inventions. A loyal customer will feel very valued if they are asked to attend a focus group reviewing your latest new product range or new gadget.

Understand how your customers are shopping and develop your offer to meet that growth.[34] Whether that is social media, mobile commerce, kiosk shopping etc., find out where they want to buy your products and how they want to buy them.

Ultimately, a good relationship with your customer can mean that they will invent your new product range for you. Remember all you are trying to do is provide the customer with what they want, when they want it and at the price they are willing to pay – if you find out what they want for the future you can go and develop it for them.

Build and live your brand

Your brand and culture runs through everything you do, have done and will do, it is the unseen 'glue' that binds your business together. Making your brand strong, and 'living and breathing', is the key to a successful and sustainable future.

[34] Join in Twitter conversations about Retail - All subjects are listed at the end of the chapter.

Summary

- *Make your business's foundations strong*
- *Network and build connections*
- *Understand what works and do more of it*
- *Utilise new technologies*
- *Grow your business with your customers*
- *Build and 'live' your brand*

 Join in the conversations about Retail on Twitter by using:

Retail is a massively competitive market, but is full of many opportunities that have been missed by the larger retailers #retailinspector [31]

Networking and building your connections is a very important skill to master when you are in business #retailinspector [32]

Think outside the box and develop new and innovative solutions for your products and services #retailinspector [33]

Understand how your customers are shopping and develop your offer to meet that growth #retailinspector [34]

10 | Build a strong foundation
for growth

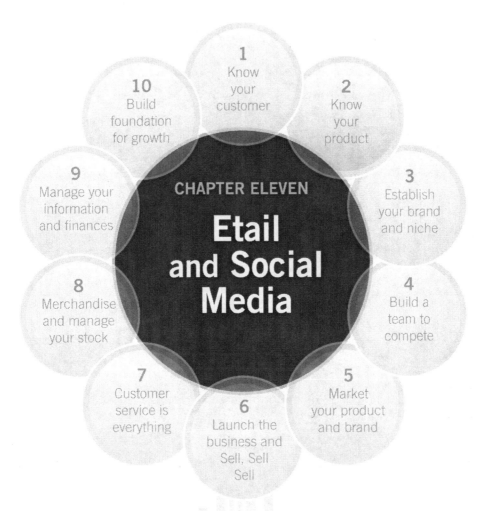

10
Build
foundation
for growth

1
Know
your
customer

2
Know
your
product

9
Manage your
information
and finances

CHAPTER ELEVEN

Etail
and Social
Media

3
Establish
your brand
and niche

8
Merchandise
and manage
your stock

4
Build a
team to
compete

7
Customer
service is
everything

6
Launch the
business and
Sell, Sell
Sell

5
Market
your product
and brand

The
Retail
Handbook

Helping you achieve your **Potential** in **Retail**

11 | 'Etail' - Set up an online store and become multi-channel

Retail has changed unrecognisably in the last few years and we have now seen a few years of strong growth in, and the emergence of, E-commerce – the selling of products to customers via the internet. There are many names for this: online shops, internet shops and E-commerce are the main names used.

I have been part of the 'internet revolution' from the late 1990s when I was lucky enough to have an internet connection at my university dormitory.

It was during this time that I realised that internet retailing has always been in retail ... R...etail..... Remove the R and you have the word 'etail' [35] – so it has always been a part of retail, we just never noticed it.

'Etail' is extremely important, and I would now say a pre-requisite for any serious retailer.[36] Whatever you sell and wherever you sell it you must have a website and you should have a transactional E-commerce website.

The world of E-commerce has changed since the growth of Amazon in the 1990s, and the realisation by retailers all across the world that the internet offers a new and exciting channel to make additional sales to new customers you would never have reached in the past.

Becoming a multi-channel retailer is the most important element of all current successful retailers.[37] Multi-channel retailing is the supply of products to your customers via many different channels, with the main

[35-37] Join in Twitter conversations about Retail - All subjects are listed at the end of the chapter.

137

channels being: a physical store, an E-commerce website and a call centre (plus new technologies and channels that are emerging).

I cannot stress how important an E-commerce website will be to grow all successful retailers. A true multi-channel retailer will be able to thrive and succeed in the competitive world we live in. In order to help you understand this better, and the opportunities you can gain from a good E-commerce website, this is discussed in the Online Retailer Case Study in this book. Here I discuss how we set up an internet-only retailer and the success of this business, which managed to sell our products in many countries around the world in a short space of time.

Without the internet channel, we would not have been able to sell FreshMax Shirts across the world. We would also have missed the opportunities to sell our fabric and technology into existing retailers all over the world if we had not launched and sold the shirts online in the first place, and made people aware of the fabric, the shirts and the brand.

Reading the case study will give you the real life secrets of the power of the internet, not only in selling your products, but allowing many other business opportunities to come to your business, taking you to places that you never dreamed you could reach.

This handbook is designed to give you an overview of what to do and what to look for when you are in the process of setting up and running an E-commerce website. It gives you an understanding of what to do and what to look for.

In future guides from The Retail Inspector, we will talk you through etail in greater depth, including: how to set up, run and make a success with a multi-channel retail business; discussing the process in depth including social media, M-commerce, the minefield of marketing options available; and the international potential your business has online.

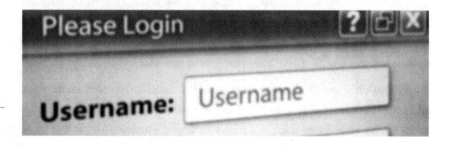

Increased ability to compete by being online

Setting up an E-commerce website will open up channels and opportunities that you would have never expected would be available to your business as a physical retailer only. The internet is 24/7 and available across the world – the potential market for your business, product and brand is truly global – there are no borders to the internet (apart from a few restricted countries).

You will be able to reach a wider local market i.e. more people in your town, district, and even country, as well as a wider world market. This potential gives you the opportunity to grow your business in ways that you had never dreamed of growing it.

More customers will see your brand and your products, thus giving you a wider customer base on which you can sell more products and make more customers happy.

You must be multi-channel in your vision for your E-commerce channel. This means that you must view your physical stores and your website in exactly the same way – they are two different 'routes' to the same business. They sell the same products, to the same customer segment, in the same way – the only difference is the medium the customer uses to interact with your business and the delivery methods.

How a multi-channel approach helps you compete:

▽ *Allows a world-wide market potential for your products and brand*

▽ *Opens up markets and customer segments you never thought you could reach*

▽ *Allows you to grow your business and therefore get better buying prices and be more competitive than your competitors*

▽ *Allows you to disseminate much more information to your customers about your brand and products*

▽ *Enables the customers to interact with your brand – to understand the stories behind the business and engage in discussion with your business*

▽ *Give you the ability to grow your product range*

▽ *Gives you a new marketing channel*

You already have the resources in your current business (if you already operate a physical store)

This is the best part of the story – you already have a retail store, so you already have everything you need to set up an E-commerce website. You do not need a massive capital investment and the months of planning and building that you would have to do if you were to build a new store.

An E-commerce site costs a few thousand pounds and takes a few months to build, and you have all the elements you need to start this now. You already have:

▼ *Product range and catalogue*

▼ *A brand and an identity*

▼ *Supply chain and warehousing*

▼ *A team to help move the products*

▼ *Marketing plans and promotional strategies*

▼ *An existing customer database and target segment*

These are all the elements you need to set up an E-commerce website. You need to find a few partners who are experts in their fields and you can then start.

The best way to do this is ask questions within your network. You may also find a competitor's E-commerce website that fits your wishes and ask them who they use to develop their web offering. They may not tell you, but you could ask them, and then research the details online if they do not tell you straight away.

What you need to start:

▼ *Your product range and catalogue hierarchy*

▼ *Information about your products, especially your USP*

▼ *Photography of your products*

▼ *Your current or planned advertising plans and artwork*

▼ *Space for the products' dispatch i.e. a store room where you can collate the orders and package them for the customers*

▼ *A laptop or computer and a connection*

As I mentioned before, this handbook is not designed to talk you through the whole process of setting up and running an E-commerce site; it gives you an overview of what to do and what to look for.

Use the internet to market your business

Using the internet for marketing a physical retail outlet has been common for the last few years, but the overwhelming customer expectation is that they want to shop and buy products online. Therefore you need an E-commerce website which is part of your multi-channel strategy to market and grow your business.

An E-commerce website offers a global market potential;[38] you can market your product to (nearly) every country in the world, and target within that market specific customer segments that you have identified as important to your business.

This will give you the opportunity to sell many more products to new customers, and also develop and grow your product range as your customers' needs and desires for your products grow.

The multi-channel approach would mean that you should use the website as a transactional E-commerce profit-making business, but also look at the website as a 'window' into your store. Your physical store window will be used to market and promote your business; think of the website front page in the same way – let customers see into your business and make them excited about your brand and your products.

Online marketing

A great marketing opportunity for a multi-channel retailer is to allow the website to give your customers 'sneak peeks' and insights into your business and your plans for the future. You can do this by many methods which are cheap and impactful when you have a great E-commerce site.

The differing forms of marketing online that you need to be aware of:

The basic element to get right from the start is <u>SEO (Search Engine Optimisation)</u>. This is where you ensure that your website is well-ranked in the search engines, i.e. when you type your product or service into Google you want to be one of the first companies in the list offering the product.

[38] Join in Twitter conversations about Retail - All subjects are listed at the end of the chapter.

An example of a search for 'Sweat-free Shirts'

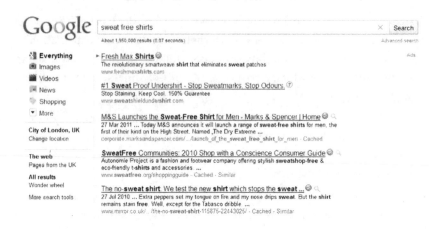

The paid-for advert is FreshMax and the first non-paid advert is the Marks and Spencer shirts, who had just launched the range and were developing their own SEO scores.

This is an important part of the design and build phase when you set up the website, and also should then be part of an ongoing strategy to ensure you are always easily found when your current and prospective customers type in your product name.

Search engines are very powerful and the larger retailers spend millions on SEO strategy – you will not be able to compete with them directly, but there are many ways you can improve your rankings in much simpler ways.

A few examples would be: making sure the names of the pages reflect the products you are selling; ensuring your website is full of relevant content to your product; you have a link-building strategy (where you link to other websites and they link to your website); building credibility of your brand on the internet – using videos is a great way to engage your customers and build good SEO rankings.

There are many more ways to improve this which are discussed in other The Retail Inspector products.

Paid for advertising – mainly known as PPC (Pay Per Click) – This is advertising on the search engines (like Google) and paying every time a person clicks on your links. This can be very successful, but also very expensive if poorly implemented.

The best way to approach this is to understand what words your customers search for when they look for your company, and then build an intelligent process to capture these searches and visits.

Remember, the aim of a search engine is to give the user the most relevant result they are looking for. Therefore, the more relevant you make your website and your PPC campaign, the more relevant customers you will receive, and the cheaper those customers will be to acquire.

The social media sites, Facebook and Linkedin in particular, have started to allow much more advertising on their websites and this can be much better quality and much more relevant to your products. It is important to make sure you put in place a comprehensive strategy for paid-for advertising, alongside the other forms of marketing we have discussed.

Direct advertising and adverts – This is when you set up an advert directly on a website and pay for the placement of this advert. There are many forms of this, with the most common being forums, entertainment sites and the popular news sites, where they have regular customers visiting. It is exactly the same as advertising in a newspaper or magazine, it is just on the screen using different images such as sky scrapers, text boxes and banners.

Affiliate marketing – This is where you allow another website to market your product to their customers in return for a commission payment. The advertiser (your business) would pay a publisher (the business with the customer's information you wish to approach) a commission for referring a customer who ultimately purchases one of your products.

The process can be operated through three main channels;

- ▼ *Adverts on publishers' sites (they would look the same as a direct advert)*
- ▼ *An email sent to a customer database the publisher owns, that has a number of customers that fit your target customer segment profile*
- ▼ *A loyalty programme, whereby the publisher runs a scheme that offers customer incentives to purchase your products via their website*

Marketing an E-commerce website has many benefits over physical marketing;

1. **Generally cheaper** – *more cost-effective.*

2. **Measureable** – *you can track the people who look at the advert or read the email and then purchase from you.*

3. **Has a very wide reach** – *the world is the customer base.*

4. **Complements** *any offline marketing strategy.*

A multi-channel strategy needs to adopt a total marketing plan – you must ensure you view the marketing of the physical retail store and the E-commerce website the same; they are different mediums, but the overall theme, messages and brand must be the same. This will ensure the customer understands your business and knows how all your channels interact as one seamless business.

Deliver total customer experience and service

A multi-channel retail offer will be expected by all customer segments, whether old or young, male or female. A large proportion of the population now uses the internet regularly and a large proportion shops for many different products online.

Offering an E-commerce website will enable you to grow with your customer and help improve their lives. We all know that people are getting more and more pressured for time and having convenient shopping options is very important. Your customers now want to shop 24/7 and they want to shop on their terms and when they want.

An E-commerce website fulfils these needs – the website is open 24/7 and allows them to interact with your business as if they were in your stores, whenever they want to and at their convenience. This will mean your customers will be happier and more satisfied with your business.

An integrated multi-channel operation will enable you to grow your product range more than you can in a physical retail store.[39] In a physical outlet you are limited by space – there are only so many products you can

[39] Join in Twitter conversations about Retail - All subjects are listed at the end of the chapter.

put into the store. Online, your only limit is your brand and what your customers want to purchase from your business.

Any new product ranges that are online-only must compliment the core range and adhere to your brand values. You will not succeed if you add products that are not relevant to your customer segments and you will be left with stock that does not sell.

When you set up the multi-channel operations, you should ensure that all your customer data is integrated. A customer does not care what channel they shop in with you, they want to ensure that they are served at the same standard each time. You can use the data from your physical store and your online store to understand how they shop and use each channel – very powerful information for future product planning.

Social Media

Social media has been spearheaded by Facebook and has become the term used to describe the way that we interact socially on the internet, using different types of conversations and discussion mediums.

Social media is now extremely important to all businesses across the world, whether they use the internet or do not use it. Your customers will use the internet to talk about your company and interact with your company whether you want them to or not. The customer is now in control of communication about your business and your brand.

You cannot control social media, but you can listen to it and use it to develop your business.[40] Being proactive with social media is very important and needs to be addressed quickly.

Social media is a great way to interact with your customers 24/7, across the world. You can form communities of like-minded customers and discuss with them new ideas, products and deal with any concerns and issues they may have.

It is important to use social media to 'listen' to what is being said about your brand and business. There are many different ways to do this which we discuss later. Not only can you 'listen' to your customers via social

---

[40] Join in Twitter conversations about Retail - All subjects are listed at the end of the chapter.

media, you can also connect with them 24/7 wherever they happen to be. This is very powerful to keep your customers up to date with what is happening in your business, be that a problem you need to let them know about (i.e. the website is undergoing maintenance for a couple of hours) or a new product launch that you would like them to come to and discuss.

Great use of social media will allow you to interact with your customers and help sell the story of your products and brand. For example, YouTube is a video channel where anybody can upload and view videos. You could use this channel to introduce your brand and company, and discuss the latest benefits of your products.

People are now connected to the internet 24/7 and often use mobile devices to connect. These allow many promotional opportunities to be gained while customers are out shopping and in the mood to buy products.

The most important tip for social media is to target the correct media channels and develop an informative and interactive communication strategy. This engages and drives the customers to a deeper understanding of your brand and ultimately drives them to purchase more products from you.

The main types of social media:

▼ *Social media websites (Twitter, Facebook, Linkedin, YouTube and Slideshare are some of the main websites) - using these social media sites will help to make people aware of you and your products and in some cases there is the ability to advertise directly*

▼ *Blogs – blogging is when anybody writes something related to your company and posts it online to create interest and awareness. There are many forms, and they can be adverts, but their main purpose is to build credibility and brand awareness*

▼ *Articles – writing an article on your area of expertise and sending it out on your website to build awareness and credibility. There are many ways to then distribute this further such as News Hubs etc.*

The E-commerce website set-up checklist

There are many parts to developing a great E-commerce website and I list the main components here. This is by no means comprehensive, but gives you a good understanding of the main areas.

- ✓ Simple, easy to read layout and colour scheme
- ✓ Easy to navigate and allows your customers to find what they are looking for easily
- ✓ Clear understanding of what you sell
- ✓ Search, Checkout and Menu bars – easy to find
- ✓ Social media icons – for easy access to your social media channels
- ✓ Logical products catalogue
- ✓ Good quality photography that shows your products in their best view
- ✓ Easy and quick checkout process
- ✓ Delivery information and costs
- ✓ Data protection and secure payments information
- ✓ Any trust or quality standards you or your product range may have
- ✓ Clear policies and terms and conditions

 Join in the conversations about Retail on Twitter by using:

Internet retailing has always been in retail ... R...etail..... Remove the R and you have the word 'etail' #retailinspector [35]

'Etail' is extremely important, and I would now say a pre-requisite for any serious retailer #retailinspector [36]

Becoming a multi-channel retailer is the most important element of all current successful retailers #retailinspector [37]

An E-commerce website offers a global market potential #retailinspector [38]

An integrated multi-channel operation will enable you to grow your product range more than you can in a physical retail store #retailinspector [39]

You cannot control social media, but you can listen to it and use it to develop your business #retailinspector [40]

Summary

- *Increase your ability to compete by being online*
- *You already have the resources in your current business (if you already operate a physical store)*
- *Use the internet to market your business*
- *Deliver total customer experience and service*
- *Understand and embrace social media*
- *Utilise the E-commerce website set-up checklist*

11 **'Etail' - Set up an online store and become multi-channel**

CASE STUDY ONE

The Online Retail
Case Study

The
Retail
Handbook

Helping you achieve your **Potential** in **Retail**

The Online Retail Case Study

The purpose of this case study is to talk you through the process we used to launch FreshMaxShirts.com and SmartWeave. The company was brand new to the market, with an exclusive new product. The challenge was that the company was unknown and had a breakthrough technology product which people did not know existed or believed could work when they heard about it.

The journey started in 2009, eight years after the founders had started to develop a cotton fabric that did not show sweat patches. A high-quality cotton fabric, which was made from 100% cotton, which felt like and acted like any high-quality premium cotton fabric. By 2009 the USA patent was granted and the rest of the world patents, including the UK and Europe, were pending. By this stage, hundreds of metres of fabric had been developed and tested; finally we had a fabric we could make into a men's shirt.

In late 2009 we set up a trading company whose purpose it would be to 'Sell FreshMax Shirts online and commercially prove the technology and the fabric'.

The journey was challenging, and we had many pitfalls to conquer and decisions to make – I describe the main part of the journey now and the ultimate results for the business.

New Brand, New Name, New Product

In 2009 we already had the name 'FreshMax', and we had a blue and white logo designed a few years previously. This logo was used solely in the discussions with other retailers, whilst attempting to persuade them to sell our SmartWeave fabric in their shirts.

151

We quickly realised we needed a totally new brand and in the beginning we thought we wanted a new name and brand. The previous image was 'sterile' and did not stand for anything – it was literally the name written in blue and white. The imagery and brand values were business- and technology-focused – we needed a high-quality, customer-facing brand.

How we did it:

We tested the idea of a new brand and new name with a number of different agencies, and some even came up with new names for the business, but we quickly realised we were best to stick to the original name and develop a new brand image and values for FreshMax.

Eventually, we employed a creative agency whose brief it was to create a customer-facing brand for FreshMax and help explain the difference between the fabric business and the FreshMax brand as a shirt company.

The main goal was to keep the fabric brand separate from the shirts brand, so that we could sell the fabric to other retailers. The creative agency soon came up with 'FreshMaxShirts' for the shirts and 'SmartWeave' for the fabric.

During a two-week process, we talked about what we wanted from the brand and what our target market looked like. We had images and talked about what the customers' life was like, i.e. where they shopped, where the worked, their hobbies and the newspapers they read. From this, the creative team presented three possible images and logos for FreshMaxShirts and the one we use now immediately made the right impression with all three directors.

A logo was developed with the 'Max' part of the brand and an entire brand image started to develop. We also chose a number of real-life images

of men in situations that we would see our customers in, to help define the final imagery and brand values.

Over the following few months we developed a set of Brand Guidelines that covered:

- ▼ **Our Brand** – *An introduction to the brand and what it was introducing to the world*

- ▼ **Before and After** – *What the world was like before the brand was developed and what the brand will bring to the world*

- ▼ **The Brand Proposition** – *An explanation of the product ranges and a brief outline of their USP*

- ▼ **The Brand Impact** – *The impact and level we were trying to achieve via the brand*

- ▼ **Our Customers** – *The types of customers our brand targets and some information about them*

- ▼ **The Brand Statement** – *The words used to describe the brand to the outside world*

- ▼ **Tone of Voice** – *How we should communicate with our customers and business partners*

- ▼ **Brand Name Usage** – *How and where we could use the brand name and in what formats*

- ▼ **Brand Phrases** – *These are statements that help people understand the brand and what it stands for*

- ▼ **Brand Values** – *The deep values and meanings of the brand*

- ▼ **Brand Appearance** – *What the brand should look and appear like in all its differing uses*

- ▼ **Visual Identity:**

    The logo – *the use of the logo in all its allowable formats*

    The colour schemes and palettes

    Exclusion zones – *where the logo should not be used*

    Imagery – *the photography and images that should be associated with the brand*

All of this work was documented in the Brand Guidelines which was then used to brief all the partners of our business. From the advertising agency to the shirt manufacturers, we made sure all the business partners understood the brand values and, more importantly, who our target customer was.

Set up and develop the website

Once we had developed a brand name and image, we needed to start the process of building a brand new website from scratch. The website had to appeal to our target customers and had to encompass the latest developments in the online shopping experience.

Due to the start-up stage we were at, we also needed to rein in our ambitions and make sure the website was developed at the best value for the money we could afford, whilst setting up a brand and image that we wished to grow and develop.

The website had to address:

Customer facing needs:

▼ *Have a one-page, easy-to-use checkout*

▼ *Compatible with all browsers and latest releases*

▼ *Be customer-friendly and easy to navigate*

'Back-end' needs:

▼ *Hold stock figures and manage the stock process*

▼ *Allow for offers and promotions*

▼ *Hold customers' details*

▼ *Upgradable for new technologies*

▼ *Allow an email database to be built and used regularly*

▼ *Integrated with the banks and secure online payment providers*

▼ *Ship to different countries*

▼ *Charge in different currencies*

▼ *Be simple for all the teams to operate and use*

The Online Retail Case Study

How we did it:

We found a partner agency who worked with us to design the 'wire frame'. A wire frame is a description of all the website pages, all the functionality and a diagram depicting the main areas and imagery on the website.

Once this was developed, the creative agency and the web partner worked together on the final designs and imagery. Many emails and meetings later, we had a website that was customer-facing and met the requirements for our brand and image.

The website was changed over the first few weeks, but started life like the above picture.

The back end of the website was built, and the system was integrated into the payment system and the bank accounts. Stock was loaded on to the system, and we had our first range of shirts arriving from Morocco to be photographed for the website.

It was all a big rush in the end, and we were still working on the website the night before the launch date – even though we had planned this for over six months.

Develop a supply chain

In late 2009 we had a manufacturing partner in France that we knew could make the fabric for the shirts (this took two years of development for them to perfect the fabric manufacturing process), but we did not have a shirt manufacturer, and at that stage we had only ever made a few test shirts. We had to start work on the supply chain alongside the development of the brand and the website.

We engaged with the French team and soon narrowed down Romania and Morocco as the best places to manufacture good quality men's shirts. We arranged a visit to four Moroccan factories and four Romanian factories in early 2010. Following these visits, we asked four factories for a full sample and a full costing – the shirts must be manufactured in a certain way and must use certain processes, and we needed to test whether the suppliers could make the shirts to our high specifications.

The process was very challenging; we had less than six months to make a full range of brand new shirts, using a brand new supply chain and fabric. The French team took full control of the sourcing and supply chain and helped us agree with a Moroccan partner for the first range and first order for delivery to our customers.

We now had a partner, but no shirt design or cut. In spring 2010 we went to Morocco with a number of shirts and in two days we developed and designed the new FreshMax Shirt fit and style. This was difficult because we knew we were selling the shirts in the UK and Europe and needed a 'European' fit.

We now had the style of the shirt and left the French team managing the manufacture and finishing of the fabric needed for launch, and the process to book and manufacture the shirts in Morocco.

The sourcing strategy we had planned and agreed meant that we would also use the French partners for the warehousing and dispatch.

The Online Retail Case Study

Pricing and promotional strategy

We kept the promotional and pricing strategy very simple from Day One; we wanted a premium shirt available to the middle market. This reflected the uniqueness of the shirt and the quality of the fabric and manufacturer.

We researched the target customer to understand the types of shirts they wore, and the types of shops they visited to purchase their shirts.

How we did it:

We identified our competitors and reviewed their pricing strategies. We knew we had a unique benefit, so we priced high so that we could compete with a 20%-off promotion. All our shirts are the same price in the UK and we set differential pricing in Europe, USA and Rest of the World.

The pricing policy was to remain simple and offer a promotional offer for the important periods and for new launches etc.

All our financial models and projections were based on a 20%-off retail price. We used the 20% for the launch and special periods and for the rest of the periods we used partner and affiliates offers to help drive sales and raise awareness.

Develop a marketing strategy

This was a major challenge and we had two main problems here:

1. *Nobody had ever heard of a shirt that does not show sweat patches.*
2. *Sweat is a very negative issue that we needed to talk about without offending our customers.*

How we did it:

The creative partners were also part of the marketing team and led the marketing planning for us. We spent a few days discussing what we should say about the shirt, breaking the functions of the shirt down into benefits for our target customer segment.

We defined our target market as: A shirt wearer in the South East, aged 25–50 years, works in an office and wants to look his best all the time.

We had to segment the market, in order to start a marketing campaign and be able to sell to our first customers. In theory the shirt should be available for every man and woman in the world, but we needed to target a very defined market in the beginning.

From this segment, we defined it further and focused our entire launch campaign on the London office workers in Canary Wharf. We realised that there are over one million men in that area each day. Concentrating on launching the business in such an area would be the most efficient and effective plan.

The message and brand strapline took a few weeks to develop. We had to be very careful about mentioning 'sweat' as it is a personal and emotional word, but the benefit of our shirts was that you did not show sweat patches and therefore the shirt was great for all men – and we needed to tell them this.

The discussion always led us to the benefits being 'improved confidence'; if you have sweat patches you notice it and you are aware of it. This makes you less comfortable and in turn less confident. A scientific study also showed us that once you are aware of sweating you sweat more – we knew we had to talk about how the product made the customer feel 'confident and free'.

We eventually decided on the strapline:

'Show nothing but confidence'.

This encapsulated all we wanted to say about the benefits of the shirt; it was our strapline at launch and still is to this day.

We also developed a sentence that described the shirts – we had to say what they were so that the customers could understand the product.

We used:

'The only shirt that eliminates sweat patches'.

This strong sentence was important to explain what a FreshMax Shirt was and why you should buy it – it describes our USP.

The next stage was to develop the adverts and these had to centre on sweat, but not the negative images of sweat – we needed 'confident and free' images and statements.

We used two of our brand images of the customers and made two separate adverts based on improving your confidence:

1. *Meeting the Board? No Sweat – A confident man with his arms back looking like he is the most confident person in the board room.*

2. *First date nerves? No Sweat – A very happy young man with*
   his arm around a beautiful girl, looking and feeling very content
   without any sweat patches.

The adverts had a theme that highlighted an occasion when you would feel nervous and start to sweat more than normal, and ended with 'No Sweat' as this was what the shirt provided the customer. A great benefit of 'No Sweat' was that its second meaning is to relax and take it easy – this was exactly how our customers wanted to feel in a stressful situation.

The adverts were now agreed and we set up the Marketing and Advertising campaign. This was very simple: Focus on Canary Wharf and London commuters.

We launched in July 2010 with paid-for advertising:

▼ *City AM (London City based free newspaper)*

▼ *The Metro (the free London commuter paper – mainly given out*
　at tube stations where it is very hot and sweaty in the summer)

▼ *A two-week poster campaign in Canary Wharf (With the 'Board*
　Meeting? No Sweat' tagline as we were targeting the office workers
　in the Canary Wharf complex)

▼ *A massive PR campaign*

Launch and PR

Launching and PR for our product was the most important area to get right, as we were a new technology product retailer, and also the area where we were likely to get the most success if we got it right. We had to develop a PR programme that would launch a totally new brand and totally new technological product to the whole world, but focusing on the target customer in UK and London.

How we did it:

We found a great PR partner, who had previous experience launching new products to the market, and also knew the press and TV contacts we needed for our product. We worked with the PR partner, advertising partner and creative partner to agree a plan to launch the product in July 2010.

The plan was based on two stories:

1. *The product technology itself and what the benefits of the world's first shirt to eliminate sweat patches would be.*

2. *The development story of two young English guys who spent eight years developing the technology.*

The plan was set up to send the PR introduction sheets to the press, magazines, TV, bloggers etc. and then follow up with meetings and product samples.

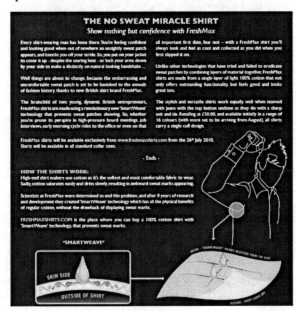

The PR campaign was a massive success, and on the day of launch the inventors appeared on ITV1 with an interview and a full two-minute test of the product. In the video, the ITV presenter wore the shirt on a bike and in a sauna, proving the technology worked. This was the perfect start to the business launch and helped prove that the shirts really do exist and they do stop sweat patches showing – even in a sauna.

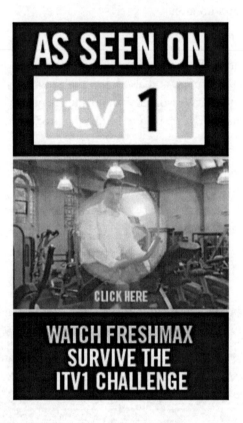

That was followed by the BBC Sunday morning show, discussing the product and again testing the product on the show. The press and magazines coverage then took hold of the story, and we were in most of the main newspapers and magazines during the first six months of launch.

A massive turning point for the business was a Reuters TV interview with the inventors. Filmed over a couple of days, this turned into a Reuters video that was sent out to over 200 countries. It was immediately picked up on news channels in the Czech Republic and Sweden. Subsequently it was found in the news in Indonesia and India.

The Online Retail Case Study

By January 2011 we had PR coverage in all national UK newspapers, BBC and ITV1, Reuters news networks, a large number of magazines and international coverage including a Sunday newspaper in Australia and a fashion magazine in the USA.

The physical launch was followed up by a massive online campaign. Using social networks (Facebook, Twitter and YouTube) we set up a two-month campaign, which made sure the news was sent out on a regular basis – mainly links to the TV and newspaper articles.

We also commissioned a video to be filmed, and set up to become a 'viral' campaign on the internet, to create a fun image with our shirts.

We filmed a Boris Johnson (the Mayor of London) look-alike, wearing our shirts and riding a TFL bike. We used a stunt bike rider to perform stunts and sent the video to many blogging sites, who in turn used the social media channels to 'viral' the video.

Customer service and fulfilment

The customer service was key to providing a high-quality service that matches the image and the brand values. This had to be done to a high standard, but also be based on a start-up budget.

The fulfilment, warehousing and dispatch were to be handled by our French partners, who would take the orders off the system twice a day and dispatch directly from France.

The customer service was to be via email and a call centre to handle the queries and reply to customers within a reasonable timescale.

How we did it:

From the start of the planning, we set up an area in the French warehouse to manage the FreshMax Shirts stock and dispatch process. A system was developed to print labels and invoices, to ensure we could pick and pack the shirts for each customer and send them ASAP.

We negotiated a contract with the French postal service that meant the costs were reasonable, and we could track all our deliveries to our customers. If we needed to send the shirts fast we used a courier.

The call centre was outsourced. They were trained and given access to the systems, to track orders and answer basic queries. Any more difficult queries were escalated to the FreshMax UK team for answering.

An email template system was set up to answer the basic customer queries in a quick and efficient process. The FAQ's section of the website covered most basic questions, but was updated as new common questions were being asked by the customers.

Returns were handled by the FreshMax UK team and managed via communications with the French warehouse team, making sure they were handled quickly and efficiently.

The results

The FreshMaxShirts.com journey was nine months from initial idea to launch day – this was very fast and involved many people and a massive investment in time and resources.

The launch was a major success with the TV and press PR, backed up by advertising in London, which meant a very good beginning for the new technology product and the E-commerce website.

Licensing the technology

Once the fabric and technology was commercially proven, the business was then able to grow the licensing part of the business, under the brand name of FreshMax Shirts in a number of countries. In these countries, expert retailers would buy the finished shirts and sell them via their own networks using their local knowledge of the retail markets.

This is an excellent way to grow a retail business into countries where you do not have the local expertise and do not know how the customers in that market respond to your products.

This was then followed by own-brand licensing and fabric deals, the first of which being Marks and Spencer PLC. Since April 2011, the shirts have been available in Marks and Spencer PLC, using the technology of FreshMax Shirts and branding them as 'Dry Extreme Shirts' by Marks and Spencer.

Dry Extreme Shirts
Our innovative shirts use SmartWeave fabric
technology to keep you and your clothes
dry and smart all day long

It is interesting to see that M&S used a similar branding to the original
FreshMax logo – it shows the differentiation of their business and their
target market versus those of the FreshMax Shirts brand.

The shirts can now be seen in a number of retailers across the world
and are still available at FreshMaxShirts.com.

Highlights of the success

▼ *Successful launch of FreshMax Shirts as a brand and launch
of SmartWeave as the fabric technology was achieved in only
nine months*

▼ *Sales in over 24 countries across the world,
including Australia and USA*

▼ *TV coverage across the world*

▼ *Press coverage across the world*

▼ *Social media coverage in many countries and many
different languages*

▼ *Successful advertising campaign in London and many
people still recall the adverts from the Metro*

▼ *New products in the pipeline
(including Linen, Women's and Trousers)*

▼ *Global sales of the fabric direct to retailers*

The Retail Handbook

FRESHMAXSHIRTS

CASE STUDY TWO

The Culture and Values Development Case Study

The
Retail
Handbook

Helping you achieve your **Potential** in **Retail**

The Culture and Values Development Case Study

The purpose of this case study is to talk you through the process we used to launch a customer-focused Shared Service Centre (SSC) in the Czech Republic.

Providing good customer service is critical to successfully operating a business as large and complex as a multi-national retailer. As part of its drive to improve customer satisfaction, the business created an SSC for the finance function.

The SSC is not directly interacting with the customer, but the SSC was part of the retail operation and, as such, had to provide excellent customer service.

Develop a Shared Service Centre

The SSC was set up to provide financial services across several European Countries and was located in Brno, Czech Republic. It had to service other companies within the group, across Europe, and had to provide the same customer service expected from its own retail stores.

How we did it:

To achieve the required standards of customer service, the SSC needed to provide high-quality team members who could understand our customers' needs, across a wide variety of tasks and countries.

This could have been a problem in Brno, where neither spoken English nor the UK business culture was in large supply. To overcome the language hurdle, it was deemed crucial that the leadership team spoke excellent English, and that the customer-facing teams spoke good English.

The rest of the team possessed intermediate English skills. Importantly, language training was offered at all levels, dependent on the needs of the individual and their role in the business.

In order to attract the type of excellence we were looking for in the teams, we offered a competitive remuneration package, comprehensive training (including English language), retail discounts and other international company benefits.

This helped drive high-performance behaviour, as a result of the higher standard of team member attracted to the company.

Create a high-performing, customer-focused culture

The SSC was set up with a very strong customer-focused culture from the beginning. The first stage was to develop the culture we wanted for the business, and the second stage was to implement the culture and help this culture 'live and breathe'.

How we did it:

The first part of the process was to visualise and develop the culture. To do this, the HR Director, the Business Development Director and I spent one day in one of our stores.

The room we chose overlooked the sales floor, so we could see and 'feel' the heart of the business – the external customers. We then spent the first couple of hours 'brainstorming' ideas, words, sentences etc. We wrote down anything that came to mind when we thought about how we should act, feel and operate in the SSC.

After a break, we started to notice a few themes appearing and we discussed these in depth. The day was intense and the process was not easy to complete. You have to think hard about the way you want everybody in your business to act and feel, focusing on giving the customer the best service possible.

In the afternoon, three clear themes appeared and for each of these we discussed exactly what it meant in practice, and how it looked on a daily basis. This was an important step to make sure we could translate the vision into real, day-to-day behaviours.

The three core values were established for the SSC:

▼ **Provide World-Class Customer Service** - *"We will provide a world-class service to our most important customer - your customer."*

- *Everybody owns our customers*
- *We take responsibility for solving problems*
- *Right first time*
- *We take pride in our results*
- *Always striving to raise the bar*
- *We operate in a high-performance environment*
- *We take pride in our working environment*
- *We embrace the 'One team' approach in all we do*

▼ **High Performance** - *"We <u>will</u> provide a high-performance environment where we welcome change and invest time and energy in developing our people."*

- *Open two-way communication*
- *Ongoing performance reviews*
- *Pride in achievements of targets*
- *Embracing and understanding change*
- *Understanding and utilising the talents of each team member*
- *Facilitating and developing individual and team ambitions*

▼ **Understanding the value of each team member to the business** - *"Your leaders will provide energy and inspiration to make you aware of the worthwhile contribution you make to the business."*

Your leaders will …

- *Provide energy and inspiration*
- *Take pride in encouraging team spirit*
- *Set clear goals for their team*
- *Lead a team who have pride, energy and respect for their customers*
- *Make their team aware of their worthwhile contribution to the business*
- *Share information to ensure their team knows what is expected of them*
- *Provide frequent open, honest, two-way communication*

Once the values had been agreed by the senior team, we then held a discussion forum with some of our new business partners in the Czech Republic. The purpose of this was to understand if these values and working practices would be beneficial and acceptable to the normal working culture in their country.

We presented the values and ideas to a number of representatives, including a professor, a couple of business owners and a recruitment company.

The feedback was excellent, and the group thought the ideas and culture would work well for our company. An interesting outcome from this forum

171

was the approach by one of the senior managers of another business. He approached us and asked if he could work in our company, as he liked the vision and believed he could thrive in that type of culture. This was a great result and, after a thorough interview process back in the UK, we employed him and he now runs the SSC.

It was important to develop a process by which we could firstly recruit the right people for the business, and secondly develop a way to train and develop them over time.

Recruiting a good team

Once we had developed the culture and values of the business, we could then move into recruitment of the teams. This was a large task, as we had to recruit 60 team members for the launch and we were in a country where we had not done business before.

How we did it:

We decided to choose a specialist recruitment partner to fulfil the brief. The recruitment partner chosen operated more like an in-house recruitment department rather than a supplier. This was extremely important to ensure that we recruited the right kind of skills – a mix of technical skills, customer service skills, and team ethos.

We took all the members of the recruitment team through the culture training and values that we had developed; it was important that we recruited the right type of personality for the business as well as the right skills for the roles.

To ensure consistency of recruitment, we used a structured interview process, which meant every level of team member had to answer the same questions, and every type of role also had to answer the same questions. This ensured consistency across the teams and the levels of hierarchy.

Develop a process to train the team

To ensure the values were understood and 'lived' by all the team, each new employee attended a 'culture training' session, exploring what the three core values meant, and how to 'live and breathe' them.

How we did it:

We held a culture training session in the second month of the team member's time with us. The first month is busy, and learning the role is important to do first; once the person had a small grasp on the role, we could then introduce the culture and values more clearly.

The format of the two-hour, interactive session encompasses three sections:

▼ *An introduction of each of the three values*

▼ *An in-depth review of each value*

▼ *A practical discussion on each value*

For the 'understanding the value of each team member' session, employees were asked to find out from the person next to them what their 'talents' were and feed these back to the group.

As a group leader, I have found this a great exercise to discover what hidden talents I had in my team – some of which I had no idea what to do with (one team member was a 'cycle artist').

During this session, many of the team find colleagues with similar interests. This is an important part of team-building in the early weeks of your team's development – you can feel the team starting to form as groups with similar interests, then interact more with each other. This ultimately leads to improved confidence and more interaction with your customers, which is a source of important information.

The final interactive session is one I chose personally – and one which could always backfire on you as a leader. I split the group into small teams and asked them how they wanted to be led and managed. This is the most important part of the session, as it enables you to discover:

1. *If you have recruited the right people.*

2. *What you, as leaders, need to do to motivate your team.*

It also works as a convenient reminder when faced with the team's complaints regarding management style later on; you can remind them that they themselves suggested the management and leadership approach during their culture training sessions.

The Culture and Values Development Case Study

Ongoing development

Ongoing development of the culture is important for your business. In the SSC everyone had a copy of the values, constantly 'talked' the values, and related new problems back to the values.

How we did it:

The process started on the first Monday morning of each month, which we set aside for new starters. This meant that we always had a number of people starting the business together, and we took them through an all-day induction session. This covered all aspects of the business, the HR formalities and introduced the customers and our values.

At the induction stage, we also made sure each team member had the values handbook and a personal training and induction plan. This is a very simple calendar that ensured they would be trained in all the areas of their job roles necessary to provide excellent customer service and fulfil the job targets.

Each new team member was also given a buddy, who was an experienced member of the current team, and could help them with all the small issues any person has when joining a new company.

From the start of the person's time with the company, they were made aware of the PDR (Performance Development Review) process. This was carried out every six months and focused on:

▼ *What they had achieved*

▼ *What they needed to improve*

▼ *What the goals were for the next six months*

The outcomes of the development plans were reviewed by HR and this led to a number of training events and training programmes being offered. These were all designed to develop the team member which would in turn develop the business.

We also used the PDR process to link in annual pay reviews and bonus payments. If a team member had a good rating they got the average pay rise; if they had an excellent rating they got an above-average pay rise. A bad rating meant no pay rise at all.

To motivate the team and focus them on customer service, we implemented an Employee of the Month Award, where people were nominated by their peers or even by external customers.

Communication and team bonding

A vital part of a good team is great communication. We had a structured meeting process and also a number of events that made sure the whole team knew what was happening and why.

How we did it:

This started on a Monday morning at 10.00 a.m. when the leadership team met to discuss the previous week's issues and highlights, and the future plans for each team. Each team leader talked through their particular area's issues and successes and we debated any issues and concerns.

At the meeting, actions were taken. There were then weekly team meetings, for each team, to ensure these actions were filtered through to every member of the team by the end of Tuesday.

We also held team builds for each team on a yearly basis, where we would ask specialists to help us to develop each team – the team build focused on the specific development issues in each team.

Once a month we held social events for the whole company, to help promote team building and enjoy themselves outside of work. They included day trips, bowling evenings and skiing holidays. These were very popular and developed a highly-motivated and contented team.

Communication is two-way and we needed to develop a way to gather feedback from all the teams. We had a very open policy and designed the office to be open plan – there were no private offices and I sat with the leadership team. This was a very new concept for the team and they were quite nervous at first.

The main way to gain the feedback was via a monthly 'directors' breakfast'. This was open to all team members who had been in the business for over three months and was set up so that there was always one person from each team as a minimum.

The meeting was informal, with coffee and cakes, and I would update the attendees on any new information and then discuss with them how things were in the business and how we could improve things. I always ended by asking each person: "If you were me and could change anything

The Culture and Values Development Case Study

in the business, what would you change and why?" The responses varied, but some suggestions were very useful and were implemented.

The SSC was a success for the business and most importantly was a customer-focused SSC – a very unusual combination. This was recognised in the second year of operation, when the SSC was a finalist in the European Shared Service of the Year Awards.

Highlights of the success

▼ *Finalist in the European New Shared Service of the Year Awards – this showed that in only two years the company was able to develop a focus on customer service*

▼ *Keeping customer service in first place in the core values led to many improvements in business practices, and many happy customers*

▼ *The team were very motivated and customer-focused, with staff attrition being one of the lowest in the industry and region*

▼ *The ultimate success has been the growth of the centre – happy customers have meant other parts of the group became customers and the SSC is over four times the original size*

The Summary

Thank you for reading The Retail Handbook – I hope this has been of great use to you and your business. I have been passionate about retail since I was very young and I have made it my life to learn about, and be the best at, retail – this handbook helps to bring you the secrets and tips I have learnt along the way.

To learn more about the services that I and my team are able to offer your business, we have developed The Retail Inspector programme. This programme is aimed at independent retailers who would like to experience more of my retail secrets, and understand the best practice the larger retailers use.

Within this programme, there are many services we provide for your business, all of which are based on good retail practice and delivered either by me or highly-trained members of my team – we can help you with all areas of running a retail business and all our services are developed to help you achieve your potential in retail.

Please visit:

www.retailinspector.com *or*

www.retailpotential.com

for more information and advice.

At the start of the book I introduced you to the journey the book would take, and we followed this journey through the chapters to the case studies.

In the book we covered the main areas of running a retail business and you were shown how I have implemented these in the past and what the best practice within retail suggests you should do. As a final reminder these are the main areas:

▼ ***Know your customer*** – Understand your customers, know them, love them and satisfy them in every part of your business

▼ ***Know your product*** – Understand everything about your products and why your customers want, need and desire your products

▼ ***Establish your brand and niche*** – Establish a brand in a defined niche market and be known for this niche

▼ ***Build a team to compete*** – Build a high-performing customer-driven and motivated team

▼ ***Market your product and brand*** – Let people know what your product range is and why your brand exists

▼ ***Launch the business and Sell, Sell, Sell*** – Launch your business and your brand, then sell your products

▼ ***Customer service is everything*** – World-class customer service is your goal throughout the entire business

▼ ***Merchandise and manage your stock*** – Make your products look good and manage your stock as if it were cash

The Summary

▼ *Manage your information and finances* – Make sure you know where your money comes from, where it goes and stay solvent

▼ *Build a strong foundation for growth* – A strong foundation is the key to long-term success

▼ *Etail and Social Media* – etail has always been part of retail, now is the time to embrace it; make etail a major part of your future journey and success

Remember, at the heart of the book is the customer, and knowing your customer was the first chapter. All the other chapters talked about the customer and the case study even showed you how a finance operation could become a customer-focused organisation.

The purpose of the book was to look at many areas of running a retail business that would ultimately lead you to achieve a few, or even all, of these outcomes:

▼ *Improve your customer satisfaction*

▼ *Grow your product range*

▼ *Improve your sale*

▼ *Develop your team*

▼ *Sell more profitably*

▼ *Take the first steps to opening an online retail store*

I hope this handbook helped you understand the process behind these areas, and introduced you to some steps for achieving these improvements in your retail business.

I will leave you with my top tips for retail, and for business in general.

I thank you for your interest in **The Retail Handbook**.

I sincerely hope you enjoyed the book and found it added value to your business.

Remember to visit: *www.retailpotential.com* for general retail news and information and *www.retailinspector.com* for more support, help and advice, all available to help you achieve your potential in retail.

Antony Welfare
The Retail Inspector
@retailpotential.com

Top Tips

Focus on the customer and provide world-class customer service – Understand their wants, needs and desires – build your business to deliver these.

Establish your brand and values – Build a brand that has the basic values to achieve what the customer requires and clearly defines your business and its way of operating.

Establish a customer-focused culture – Build a team that lives and breathes your values, making world-class customer service the heart of every team and successfully growing your business.

Make sure quality is in everything you do – Make sure that everything you do is done to the best ability of you and your teams – always strive to give the best service every day with every person you interact with.

Reward and incentivise to develop a motivated and happy team – A motivated and happy team will lead to happy customers, which leads to success – listen to and look after your team.

Manage your cash – Cash is sanity and profit is vanity, a business will go bankrupt due to lack of cash, not lack of profit. Understand where your money comes from and where it goes.

Develop and communicate a clear vision, strategies and plans – Know what you are trying to achieve and have a plan to get there. Share the vision, strategies and plans with all your teams and partners.

Top Tips

Make your customers the heart of every team and make them feel special – Happy and satisfied customers are loyal and keep you successfully retailing.

Retail is Detail – Get the details right for the customer and look after the detail - understand what is happening and make sure you 'dot the i's and cross the t's'.

It's not rocket science – Retail is one of the oldest forms of business – we buy a product and sell it on to the end consumer with a margin; make sure that that your margin delivers a profit.

Make decisions – Just do it. Do not procrastinate; analyse the information, make decisions and give it a go – if it doesn't work, try another way.

Manage with facts and information – Use the data and information you have in your business. Keep your emotions in check and make decisions based on solid information, analysis and research.

Don't forget to sell your products and your business – After all we are in the retail business to sell products to customers – that is the reason they visit your stores and what they require from your business.

Be yourself and enjoy – this is your journey to achieving your potential in retail – make sure you take pleasure in it.

Acknowledgments

I had never planned to write a book, and without my publisher and editor I would not have written my first book that covers my lifetime of learning in retail to date.

I have always been in the retail industry and have never left it or wanted to leave. I know I will never leave the industry – it is far to exciting and motivating to ever need to leave.

There are many people that have helped me on this journey who have been fantastic and too many to mention personally. A big Thanks to you all for your help.

I have had some very important teachers during the years and the first teacher was at my local newsagent. Sam Sellers allowed me to start working in his Newsagent and trained me over a couple of years in all areas of running a retailer – from Customers to stock management. What I learnt then, has stayed with me all the way through my life, and I thank Sam for his contribution to my career.

My business mentor and friend, and the writer of the foreword of this book, Roger Best, has been a fantastic help to me in the last few years. He has helped me navigate the FreshMax journey and has made sure that all my ideas and plans are thought through and comprehensive – Thanks for your time and priceless advice.

I would like to thank my managers and teachers at Marks & Spencer, Sainsburys and Dixons Retail, who have all helped me grow my experience and become a very successful retailer. Some of my days in these companies were very hard, but the learning's from these retailers has been significant in my life.

The book has been helped along by a number of friends and business partners and I would like to thank all the reviewers – I appreciate the hours they spent reading the manuscript and I would like to thank my mum for checking the editors' edits – nothing better than your mum to cast her eye over your work!

Most importantly, I would like to thank my friends. Some have had to sit next to me on a plane, as we flew for a weekend away to Iceland, whilst I edited the book on my iPad 2, and all my friends have had to listen to many hours of stress as I sent them ideas and book cover designs! They have had to endure hundreds of Facebook and twitter updates, telling them how many words I have written and how much time I have spent writing – I know I drove them mad, but that's why they love me!

Thanks to all my friends for their love and support

If you've enjoyed **The Retail Handbook**, then please

Follow **The Retail Handbook** on twitter
@AntonyWelfare or #retailinspector

Visit **www.retailinspector.com** or **www.retailpotential.com**
for updates and free downloads

Post a review on **www.amazon.co.uk**

About the Author

Antony specialises in Retail, with over 20 years experience in the retail industry, including 15 years learning from the large retailers (Marks & Spencer, Sainsburys, Dixons Retail) and experience of smaller retailers, including the set up, and subsequent sale, of a very successful online retailer.

Starting in a newsagent at the age of 15, was when Antony fell in love with retail and this progressed throughout his life and still to this day.

Once at college he started work at Sainsbury's and soon progressed to the customer service team. With retail now firmly in his blood he went to Loughborough University to study Retail Management for 4 years, including a year in Mark & Spencer stores. This is where he started to learn the real detail of running a successful retail business. On graduation he moved to London, joining the Sainsbury's Graduate programme, spending two years at HQ in trading and property roles.

He then returned to Marks and Spencer where he spent 5 years at HQ, learning the trade in areas such as store development, buying and merchandising.

The following 5 years were spent at Dixons Retail, where he looked after the UK E-commerce sites, the Dixons chain, a B2B company and spent 2 years in the Czech Republic creating a new European Shared Service (Finalist in the European Shared Service awards). With his last role as the Commercial Finance Director for the UK.

In 2009, he left Dixons Retail to set up the retail arm of FreshMax Shirts (SmartWeave) - the world's only fabric which eliminates sweat patches.

Antony now heads up the Retail Potential company, offering Retail Consultancy and the flagship programme - The Retail Inspector programme which offers independent retailers access to the best practice from larger retailers.

 Please contact us for further information about our services and for free downloads at: **www.retailinspector.com**

 Join in the conversation **#retailinspector** – details are at the end of each chapter.

Contacts:

 antony@retailpotential.com

 AntonyWelfare

 facebook.com/AntonyWelfare

 http://uk.linkedin.com/in/antonywelfare

Testimonials

"In this comprehensive Retail Handbook, Antony covers the major challenges of running a retail business. Practical advice and examples throughout the book will help your retail business to grow and importantly focuses on the customers and the team. A great aide for all retailers"

Mark Chatterton, Group Sales and Marketing Director, Computers Unlimited

"A comprehensive guide to all things retail. Whether you have been retailing for 20 years or are just dipping your toe in the water, you'll find tips to improve your business"

Jo Illingworth, former Head of Brand Marketing, Dixons Tax Free

"Retail is more than just the product: it's the customer, the store colleagues, the service and the relationship between all of them. This book neatly pulls these elements together in a way that both the novice and the expert will find both useful and accessible"

Neil Symons, Head of HR Transformation Rollout, International FTSE 100 Retailer

"Antony's enthusiasm for retail shows as much in his writing as it does when in person - that's one helluva lot of enthusiasm. This handbook is a must for all those trying to get to grips with the quintessentials of retail - our students need one as standard issue."

Cheryl Travers, Senior Lecturer, Retail Management, Loughborough University

"Retail has been around as long as man himself, yet I'm sure it has never before been captured in such simple prose and so comprehensively. Using real life case studies this book will offer you advice to improve your retail skills."

Mark Buckley, Business Analyst, Marks and Spencer

"There is a good combination of strategy and 'nitty-gritty,' with numerous common-sense tips based on insights from Antony's retail experience. Both the planning and the execution are well covered and each section has a helpful checklist of subjects to consider. The book is possibly unique in providing such a comprehensive practical guide to retailing in one compact volume."

Roger Best, Retailer with over 20 years experience leading consumer brands and former CEO of Radley

"The passion for and understanding of retail in all its finest details radiate from this book and the author personally"

Frank Van Bommel, Training and Development Manager, Dixons Retail

Introduction to The Retail Inspector programme:

Welcome to The Retail Inspector programme, which is designed to help local and independent retailers compete with the larger "faceless" retail businesses.

The exclusive community allows independent retailers access to a number of services and a large amount of expert retail support and advice.

Independent retailers can gain access to the best retail practice and the best retail experts available via the three parts of the programme:

1. **The Retail inspector community**
2. **The Retail Inspection**
3. **The Retailing Skills Profile**

The Retail Inspector community

The main benefits of the community are:

Members only community with qualified retailers only

State of the art interactive community; offering all the benefits of the main social networking sites, but specifically for independent retailers and completely confidential

Channel networking groups - private groups of similar retailers that want to discuss ideas and themes in confidence i.e a hardware retailer in London would share secrets with a fellow hardware retailer in Scotland

Geographic networking groups - private groups of geographically based retailers that want to discuss ideas and themes in confidence, with their local retail businesses.

Plus all these added benefits for members:

▼ A **Monthly newsletter** covering the main retail news from the previous month and any **guest columns** the experts may wish to add

▼ Access to **"Ask the expert"** to ask questions and gain advice from expert retailers

▼ **Training** provided by us and partners

▼ Access to **members adverts** and **best practice**

▼ Quarterly **store visits feedback** of large retailers with a full case study and findings by the retail inspector

▼ **Best/top tips** from that months inspections from the team

▼ **Panel interview** with top retailers

▼ Entry to **"Retailer of the year" awards.**

The Retail Inspection

The main benefit of the **"Retail Inspection"** *is to improve:*

Customer Satisfaction, Sales, Profits, Cost control, Stock and Time Management.

The **"Retail Inspection"** involves a few days with one of our Retail Inspectors looking at the whole Retail experience, including customers, staff using the tried and tested **"Retail Checklist"**.

The outcome of this is **an action plan that the retailer can implement**.

The top package (Gold) even offers a **six monthly review** and **on-going support** from their Inspector.

The Retailing Skills Profile

An extremely detailed and high quality online survey that helps any retailer identify the areas that they need to improve in order to achieve **best practice**.

▼ **73 Questions of Yes/Maybe/No are weighted**
▼ **10 areas are then summarised, scored and advice given**
▼ **25 page PDF Report.**

Thanks for your interest and please contact me directly for more information on the programme.

Antony Welfare
The Retail Inspector
www.retailinspector.com
Email: antony@retailpotential.com

189

Lightning Source UK Ltd.
Milton Keynes UK
UKOW041655110213

206126UK00002B/2/P

9 781907 722363